Letters to My Children

A FATHER PASSES ON HIS VALUES

Daniel Taylor

INTERVARSITY PRESS
DOWNERS GROVE, ILLINOIS 60515

©1989 by Daniel Taylor

All rights reserved. No part of this book may be reproduced in any form without written permission from InterVarsity Press, P.O. Box 1400, Downers Grove, Illinois 60515.

InterVarsity Press is the book-publishing division of InterVarsity Christian Fellowship, a student movement active on campus at hundreds of universities, colleges and schools of nursing. For information about local and regional activities, write Public Relations Dept., InterVarsity Christian Fellowship, 6400 Schroeder Rd., P.O. Box 7895, Madison, WI 53707-7895.

Distributed in Canada through InterVarsity Press, 860 Denison St., Unit 3, Markham, Ontario L3R 4H1, Canada.

All Scripture quotations, unless otherwise indicated, are from the Holy Bible, New International Version. Copyright © 1973, 1978, International Bible Society. Used by permission of Zondervan Bible Publishers.

Cover illustration: Roberta Polfus
Calligraphy: Tim Botts

ISBN 0-8308-1264-4

Printed in the United States of America ∞

Library of Congress Cataloging-in-Publication Data has been requested.

17	16	15	14	13	12	11	10	9	8	7	6	5	4	3	2	1
99	98	97	96	95	94	93	92	91	90	89						

For Matthew, Julie, Nate, and—surprise!—Anne, with all a father's love. And for Jayne, who taught me by example what love is. And for my father and mother (and "cloud of witnesses"), who passed their values on to me.

Preface

I have a terminal disease. It is called mortality. It causes me, at times, to worry about my children growing up without me. I am not afraid they will miss meals or education or have to wear generic jeans (my oldest son's worst nightmare). I am concerned they will little remember who their father was, what made him tick, what was important to him, what he had to say to them. What will they know of me, of the man who co-created them, the one who loves them more than he will ever let himself say?

These letters are a partial response to this muted but persistent concern. They are, in theory, for my children, but in writing them I discovered they were for me, and perhaps for others, as well. It is not just the vanity of wanting to be remembered that motivates them. For better or worse, I am the only father my children will ever have. And as their father, part of my value is to pass on the eternal truths. Never mind that many of us are less sure of the exact nature of eternal truth than before we had children. Never mind that when the words come out of our mouths they sometimes sound suspiciously like clichés or, worse yet, like things we didn't like hearing from our own parents.

Despite our inadequacies, we fathers serve a crucial purpose by being there to say the expected, unexceptional, but necessary thing. *What* exactly we have to say will often be forgotten; that we are there to say it will never be. And fathers can say things mothers cannot, or can say the same thing in a way that is necessarily different. And of course the same is true for mothers, and that's why children need both their parents.

So what will happen to my children if I die before they have asked all their questions? Their mother is wonderful in every sense, but she cannot be a father. What will they remember of me? They will know that I looked a certain way, that I had such-and-such a profession, that I accomplished this or that in life. They might remember or be told that I had these traits—a sense of humor, a love of books, a fear of God—but what of my values, what of my peculiar vision of life? What, in short, of all the things that would have been communicated to them—through the ears, through the eyes, through the heart—in all those passing conversations that would have taken place over the years?

These letters are my answer. Not enough, to be sure, but it gives me comfort knowing they exist. I wouldn't want them to take the place of even one real conversation, but should they have to stand in my place, my hope is that one word is worth a thousand pictures.

Yes, these letters are for my children. But in a sense they are for me too. I had the strange experience in writing them of setting out to pass on wisdom that I discovered I did not possess. I imagined questions from them for which I did not have convincing answers. In groping around for responses I often found myself telling stories from my past. I now see a logic in this. Stories are detailed explorations of people tangled in the messiness of living. And, if it is to mean much, so is any wisdom we have to pass on to our children.

These stories come from my own past, but some of them may be from your past as well. If these letters are for me as well as for my children, perhaps they are also for you. We listen to the stories of others because they are both like and unlike our own. What stories do you have to tell? What letters do you have to write?

ONE

What Price Popularity?

Papa, this nerd
wants to sit next to me
at school. Nobody likes
him and neither do I.
What do you do
when someone who's out of it
wants to be your friend?

D ear Matthew,

THERE ARE WAYS TO BE A FRIEND TO SOMEONE
without being a bosom buddy. Even an occasional act of
kindness can change the way a person feels about life. I'm
thinking of Mary, a girl who was in my class once. But let me
tell you the story.

When I was in the sixth grade I was an all-American. I was
smart, athletic, witty, handsome (especially with a Vaselined wave
of hair sweeping back from my forehead) and incredibly nice.
Things went downhill fast in junior high, but for this one year
at least I had everything.

Unfortunately, I also had Miss Owens for an assistant teacher.
Miss Owens was a college girl who was practicing on us. She
helped Mr. Jenkins, our teacher. Miss Owens also went to my
church. She knew that even though I was smart and incredibly
nice, there was a thing or two I could still work on.

One of the things you were expected to do in grade school
was learn to dance. My parents may have had some reservations

at first, but since this was square dancing, it was okay.

Every time we went to work on our dancing we did this terrible thing. And I mean it when I say it was terrible. I hope this kind of thing isn't done anymore. The boys would all line up at the door of our classroom. Then, one at a time, each boy would pick a girl to be his partner. The girls all sat at their desks. As they were chosen, they left their desks and joined the snot-nosed kid who had honored them with his favor.

Believe me, the boys did not like doing this—at least I didn't. But think about being one of those girls. Think about waiting to get picked. Think about seeing who was going to get picked before you. Think about worrying that you'd get picked by someone you couldn't stand. Think about worrying whether you were going to get picked at all!

Think if you were Mary. Mary was a girl who sat up near the front on the right-hand side. She wasn't pretty. She wasn't real smart. She wasn't witty. She *was* nice, but that wasn't enough in those days. And Mary certainly wasn't athletic. In fact she'd had polio or something when she was small; one of her arms was drawn up, and she had a bad leg, and to finish it off, she was kind of fat.

Here's where Miss Owens comes in. Miss Owens took me aside one day and said, "Dan, next time we have square dancing, I want you to choose Mary."

She may as well have told me to fly to Mars. It was an idea that was so new and inconceivable that I could barely hold it in my head. You mean pick someone other than the best (the prettiest, most popular) when my turn came? That seemed like breaking a law of nature or something. It was like purposely trading a Mickey Mantle card for an Andy Pafko. Who wants Pafko when you can have Mantle? Who would pick Mary when there was Linda, Shelley or even Doreen?

And then Miss Owens did a really rotten thing. She told me it was what a Christian should do. I knew immediately I was doomed. I was doomed because I knew she was right. It was exactly the kind of thing Jesus would have done. I was surprised, in fact, that I hadn't seen it on a Sunday-school flannel-board yet: "Jesus Choosing the Lame Girl for the Yeshiva Dance." It was bound to be somewhere in the Bible.

I agonized. Choosing Mary would go against all the coolness I had accumulated. It wasn't smart. It wasn't witty. Maybe it was nice, but even I didn't want to be that nice.

The day came when we were to square dance again. Mr. Jenkins told Miss Owens to go up to the cafeteria to set up. Then he lined up the boys by the door.

It was worse than you think. If God really loved me, I thought, he will make me last. Then picking Mary will cause no stir. I will have done the right thing, and it won't have cost me anything.

You can guess where I was instead. For whatever reason, Mr. Jenkins made me first in line. (Had Miss Owens been talking to him?) There I was, first in line, my heart pounding—now I knew how some of the girls must have felt.

The faces of the girls were turned toward me, some smiling. I looked at Mary and saw that she was only half-turned to the back of the room, her face staring down at her desk. Mr. Jenkins said, "Okay, Dan—choose your partner!"

I remember feeling very far away. I heard my voice say, "I choose Mary."

Never has reluctant virtue been so rewarded. I still see her face undimmed in my memory. She lifted her head, and on her face, reddened with pleasure and surprise and embarrassment all at once, was the most genuine look of delight and even pride that I have ever seen, before or since. It was so pure that I had to look away because I knew I didn't deserve it.

Mary came and took my arm, as we had been instructed, and she walked beside me, bad leg and all, just like a princess. When we walked into the cafeteria, Miss Owens was already thumping out a march on the piano. She looked over at Mary and me coming in at the head of the line and she smiled real big but with no surprise at all, like she knew all along.

Linda and Shelley came up to me later and, in a catty kind of way, said, "Miss Owens made you do that, didn't she?" I said no. And I wasn't lying. Miss Owens didn't make me do it. She had asked me to do it. She had told me I should. But *I* had chosen Mary. And I was glad.

Mary is my age now. I never saw her after that year. I don't know what her life's been like or what she's doing. But I'd like to think she has a fond memory of at least one day in sixth grade. I know I do.

Love, Papa

TWO

====

Sometimes Trying
Is Not Enough

====

How come, lately,
the harder I try
the less things go right?

Dear Nate,

YOUR GRANDPA DARRELL HAD THIS PROBLEM ONCE.
When he was a kid growing up in Ventura, California, he loved
the things little kids love—and one of those things was baseball.

One spring the Chicago Cubs came to town to play an
exhibition game. Now you have to remember that this was long
before television, and there were no major league baseball teams
anywhere in the western half of the United States. This was the
chance of a lifetime not only for the little kids of Ventura but
also for many of the adults.

As if this weren't enough, Grandpa somehow got chosen,
miracle of miracles, to be the bat boy for the Cubs. No further
proof was needed that there was a good God in heaven!

Everyone of sound body and mind, and a few who weren't,
showed up at the game. And there was Grandpa in the dugout,
feeling as important as a kid could feel and still be a kid.

Everything went fine until the later innings of the game when the pitcher for the Cubs came to bat. One way or another, he got to first base. Then someone threw Grandpa a jacket and told him, "Take it to the pitcher."

I don't know whether Grandpa didn't know that in the major leagues the pitcher puts on a jacket when he gets on base, or whether he hadn't noticed that it was the pitcher who had been up to bat, or what. But instead of running to first with the jacket he ran out to the pitcher's mound and held it out.

The guy on the pitcher's mound just stared at him. Grandpa was confused. Someone in the dugout yelled again, "Take it to the pitcher." Grandpa turned and offered it again to the guy on the pitching mound.

By now some of the people in the stands behind the dugout were yelling, "Take it to the pitcher." More and more people picked it up, and soon the whole stadium, the whole town, the whole universe it seemed, was chanting, "Take it to the pitcher! Take it to the pitcher! Take it to the pitcher!"

Finally the manager came out of the dugout. He walked over to this sad little kid standing in the middle of the infield, put his arm on his shoulder, pointed to first base, and whispered in his ear, "Take it to *that* pitcher."

This is how life is sometimes. You try your best, you try to do right, but things just don't work the way you think they should. You are told to take a jacket to the pitcher and so you try to do that, but everything gets confused.

Often this happens, as it did to Grandpa as a little kid, because we think we understand what's going on and we really don't. We do things because we think the world is one way, when really it is another. (We think, for instance, that we are providing for our families by bringing home a big paycheck, and then we find out that's not what they need from us.)

If we are lucky, we have someone like that manager to come and put his or her arm around us and point us to first base.

Love, Papa

THREE

When Dogs and People Die

Papa, how come things die?
What happens to them?
Did anyone you know die
when you were a kid?

Dear Julie,

THANKS FOR FINALLY ASKING SOME EASY QUESTIONS. These aren't easy questions at all, of course—for children or adults.

Yes, things and people I knew died when I was a kid, and it was hard. The first things I remember dying were our dogs. They died regularly, whenever I least expected it. It was kind of their calling.

Our dogs were accident prone, especially around cars. The one I remember most clearly was Trumpet, one of our Texas dogs. Like all our dogs he was a mutt, and he liked to chase cars. (It doesn't seem to me that dogs chase cars as much as they did when I was a boy.) Trumpet was a runt of a dog, but after barking at the back tire of a car for half a block he would come loping back to us with a look of satisfaction on his face like he'd just conquered the Roman Empire.

The first time he got hit, it broke his back leg. The vet put a cast on it supported by a heavy wire that outlined his leg. I can still remember the sound of that wire cast hitting the hardwood floors as he patrolled the house. He even kept chasing cars with his cast on: *bark!* clunk, *bark!* clunk, *bark!* clunk. He thought he was grand and so did we.

The second time he got hit, he wasn't so lucky. The car that hit him stopped for a second and then roared away. We kids stood around Trumpet's body in the road and watched as the car disappeared. We couldn't believe somebody would kill our dog and then not even stop to say they were sorry.

I didn't cry right away. In fact, I remember that as a kid I almost never cried right away when something bad happened. At first I was mostly mad at the person who had killed my dog. Then I knew I had to get Trumpet out of the street.

So I carried him home. He wasn't a big dog, but now that he was dead he seemed the heaviest thing in the world. His body was totally limp and floppy. I felt as I carried him that I was starting to understand what death was.

It was only later, on my front porch, after I had told my parents, that I felt this kind of pressure deep down in my chest and it started rising up in my throat and I knew I was going to cry. And so I did cry, not long but hard, and I felt better.

We buried Trumpet in a vacant lot near our house. All the neighbor kids were there. We put a little flower wreath on the spot, and that seemed good.

Over the next couple of weeks I came to visit the grave every day and worried a little that the flowers themselves were dying. One day, after we started to think about other things more, a bunch of us were playing in my yard. We looked up the street to the vacant lot and saw some bigger kids digging around where the flower wreath was, probably wondering what was under it.

All the old anger at the person who'd run over Trumpet and

hadn't stopped to apologize came instantly back. We ran toward the grave, screaming and yelling, not thinking for a moment what we'd do once we got there. Amazingly, the older kids saw us coming and ran for their lives. We got to Trumpet's grave and shook our fists at them as they disappeared up the alley. We felt good about ourselves.

We got another dog and, later, he got run over too.

The first *person* I knew who died was Debbie. I was ten and I think she was twelve. She had leukemia. That's a disease of the blood that makes you get sicker and sicker until you die, not like getting run over by a car.

Debbie was kind of like an angel. She had blond hair and a real nice smile and she was funny. She knew she was dying but still she laughed a lot. I can't remember much of what I felt except that I thought she was very special. I treated her the best I could, and I remember wondering how her brother and sister could sometimes fight with her. I mean, she was *dying* and all.

But now I know they were right to fight with her sometimes. It kept her part of the family.

I don't think I cried when she died. Dying seemed to be the reason why she was here in the first place. It was the only way I had known her—as the friend who was going to die. She had, it seemed, fulfilled her calling.

The funeral didn't feel right, not as good as the one we had had for Trumpet. When we had buried Trumpet, I felt like he was there and that we were doing the right thing by him. When I looked at Debbie in that casket, I didn't feel like she was there at all. We were there, doing the things we were supposed to do, but she was somewhere else, still smiling, perhaps at us with our long faces.

A few years after Debbie died, her sister died too—leukemia again—and her brother ran away from home.

And then there was Phyllis. Ah, Phyllis! I still don't know exactly what to make of her. I was in college then, and she was dying of cancer. She was an old acquaintance of the family, having once been married to my father's college roommate. Phyllis had had a tough life, partly of her own doing, and now she was laced with cancer, sleeping in a chair, wearing a wig and waiting to die.

But with what expectation she waited! Phyllis had this sense of peace that impending death gives some people. Or probably I should say, that God gives some people when they are about to die. Or better still, that is available from God for most people if they are interested in claiming it.

Phyllis knew God. She had seen the first and the last, the beginning and the end. She knew who had made her, who had redeemed her, and who (her broken body notwithstanding) was ready to take her back to himself.

Your mom and I talked to her for long hours. Phyllis had to stop sometimes because of the pain, but she'd make us stay until the pain subsided and she could talk again. She told us pain was often a good thing. "Many good things are painful," Phyllis said: giving birth to a child, writing a poem, asking for forgiveness.

Phyllis thought it a very bad sign that Americans were so afraid of pain that they thought the worst thing in the world was to suffer. She felt suffering had brought her back to God, back to a real understanding of what was important in the world.

Phyllis claimed that the Spirit of God came to her in the night and comforted her. She said it was like a warm light and that it gave her an overwhelming feeling that all shall be well, and all manner of things shall be well.

Phyllis had no money; she was divorced and living alone; she was in constant physical pain; her precious teen-age daughter had been killed a few years earlier. It is very odd, by the world's standards, that this woman should be the most contented person I have ever known. Some people would say she had lost touch with reality in order to protect herself against its pain. I think, rather, she had gotten *in touch* with reality in a way that few of us ever do, and had seen its beauty.

So what does all this say about dying? I don't know. Maybe it says that dying is one of the things that helps us know what living is. It says that dying hurts, both those who die and those who are left behind, who will die when their turn comes. It also suggests, however, that dying may be the beginning of something rather than the end.

Some people say that when you die you just stop being and the atoms in your body simply return to the earth to form new combinations to make other things that will also die.

I don't think that is so. I think God made us and those atoms in the first place. I think he has other plans for us because he loves us. He came to Phyllis in the night because he wanted her to know he loved her and that soon she would see her daughter again, face to face.

We die because we have lived. We live in order to know and love the God who made us. In dying we become more real than we ever can be while part of this sorrowful world.

I will die someday, and so will you. And that is a good thing.

Love, Papa

FOUR

Car
Status

Papa, why do we always
drive old cars?
It's embarrassing.

Dear Matthew,

I KNOW THIS IS A PROBLEM, ESPECIALLY HERE IN the suburbs where we find ourselves for the time being. I can remember you sitting in the back seat of one of our rust-mobiles, when you were five or six, with your friend Chad.

I was driving you two somewhere and listening in on your conversation. At one point you made what sounded like a formal announcement to your friend: "When I grow up, I am going to be the first person in my family ever to own a new car." Actually it sounded more like a religious vow. Chad wasn't impressed. He replied matter-of-factly: "We always have new cars."

I'm not sure who's to blame for us not driving new cars. I could say it is because I'm a teacher and teachers aren't as valuable in America as, say, ball-bearings salesmen, and so we don't get paid much. But that's not really it. Some teachers drive new cars, and I suppose I could too if I really wanted one.

If I have to blame it on anything, I think I'll blame it on Jon. Jon was my friend of longest standing. Now I don't rate my friends, calling them "best friend" or "closest friend" or "fairly-good-friend-if-no-one-else-is-around." Friends are so fine to have at all that I don't want to diminish any of them by trying to figure out who falls where. But by any rating, Jon would be on or near the top.

I moved so much as a kid that I thought of friends sort of like a candy bar in my hand—something that was going to give me a lot of pleasure, but which I knew wouldn't be around for long. But Jon was different. He was one who stayed.

I met Jon when I was in fourth or fifth grade. He went to my church, and *looked* like a kid who went to church—skinny, tall, with a big nose, sort of shy and quiet. It seemed fitting that he was left-handed. When we played softball, Jon was always in right field. (You know what that means!)

Jon had an unusual last name. His full name was Jon Frederick Dingeldein. It sounded sort of like an ice-cream truck chiming down the street.

I think Jon's last name shaped his personality some. It made him tolerant, for one thing. How could you be hard on other people when your name was Dingeldein? A name like that left you vulnerable and perhaps a little more sensitive to the pain of others.

We went to camp together once. I remember the first night everyone had to give their name and where they were from. I recall sitting there worrying for Jon as his turn came closer. He seemed resigned. When it was his turn, he said, "Okay—my name is Jon Dingeldein. Go ahead and laugh. I'm used to it." And a few of them did, but by beating them to the punch he took away the sting.

As Jon got older, he developed a certain stubborn pride in his name. We, his friends, would sometimes while away the indolent hours of adolescence suggesting changes—"Jon Dingle," "Jon

Dein," "Jon Dingleberry." He resisted them all. It was his name and he didn't want it any different.

Jon was an ideal friend—a wonderful combination of quiet wit and gentleness. Later, under the tutelage of another friend with more primitive instincts, he discovered in himself a love of adventure. Quiet Jon could be found stalking the night, placing time-fused cherry bombs around the houses of neighborhood grouches, lurking in the bushes with a towel-rack blowgun and paper darts aimed at unsuspecting girls coming from prayer meetings. His body took on mythic proportions, and he was described to police by one distraught youth leader as simply, "The Tall."

(Don't worry—very soon I'll get to what this has to do with cars.)

By this time Jon was in college. We roomed together for a couple of years. He was tall, as always, but now he was strong instead of skinny. He was confident and smart and almost handsome, but still essentially gentle and kind. He was the type of person you felt good being around.

But Jon's body was beginning to betray him. There, beneath the tan surface and the appealing smile, were cells which followed a different drummer—cells which would eventually kill his body.

After college, Jon went unsuspectingly to medical school, and I went to learn more about words. In four years we were both doctors, but he was a real one.

And almost as soon as he was *Doctor* Jon Frederick Dingel-dein—a status we as his friends were very proud of—he found that he had cancer, melanoma. In a way, we all felt we had cancer.

Not long before he died, at the age of twenty-six or twenty-seven, we went flying model gliders on the hill above his house where his ashes were later scattered. He flew a remote-controlled glider that he had built himself, sanding with unnecessary but characteristic care parts of the glider that would never be seen.

I watched him watch the glider which he controlled with the small box in his hands. Because of the cancer, he was now skinny again—the same as he had been when he played right field. His hair had mostly fallen out. But at that moment, Jon was intent on the sweep of his plane in the sky.

Watching Jon, I knew that I didn't need new cars, although I didn't put it to myself that way then. But I knew that life was very short and very fragile. I knew that being good, loving and being loved, were no guarantee against sudden death.

I knew that we are here on this earth for something more than making money, or getting well known, or becoming powerful. Soon after Jon died I quit a job I didn't like. I decided I would take chances in my life to do things that have eternal consequences in what little time I had.

I am somewhat disappointed in myself to tell the truth. I haven't taken very many chances. I now have a job that is similar to the one I quit. I may or may not have done much that has eternal consequences. (I've quit trying to judge that.)

But I have learned not to care about new cars. I know now that all of them turn to rust, just as we do. There are other things to focus on. Jon taught me that, and I am grateful for the lesson.

Love, Papa

FIVE

Embarrassingly Human

It was terrible, Papa.
I messed up in front of everyone.
I can't show my face again.
We'll have to move to
North Dakota—tonight!

Dear Nate,

I KNOW HOW YOU FEEL. REALLY. IT'S ONE THING TO screw up—everybody does that. It's another thing to give a public demonstration in screwing up. Your mother did that once or twice. In high school she was in a school play and forgot almost *all* her lines (and she had a lot of them) in front of her parents, friends, teachers and the student body. Now there's a public embarrassment! But I'll let her tell you that one if she wants.

Maybe you'd like to hear about one of mine. I was a sophomore in high school. I played basketball on the "B" team—that is, the team composed of medium-sized runts. Our school was playing Santa Barbara High, the powerful cross-town rivals. So many people came to these games they had to hold it at the university. This basketball game was one of the big events of the year.

Now nobody usually cared about the "B" teams. But this year they decided to play the "B" game right before the varsity contest. As a result, instead of the usual one to three people watching our games, this time there were thousands. Not that it particularly affected me, since I was the original bench warmer. I could sit just as successfully before thousands as before a few.

No such luck. Somewhere in the middle of the fourth quarter, as I painfully but comfortably watched my teammates getting their brains beaten out by a bunch of high-jumping, spin-moving ghetto kids, I heard the reedy voice of Mr. Dee, our beaverish, bucktoothed, history teacher coach: "Taylor!"

His voice sounded like the call of God. I should have detected the ring of doom in it. Mr. Dee was clearly distraught at what would go down as "The Slaughter of the Runts."

"Taylor, I want you to go in there and give me everything you've got!"

It wasn't a timeless, inspirational speech but it was more than enough for me. I was ready to avenge a lifetime of sitting on assorted benches. In five minutes of brilliant play I would have my revenge on all the coaches who had looked at me and wondered why they hadn't taken that job at the auto parts store instead.

I ripped off my warm-up suit, being careful not to pull down my trunks as I pulled off my sweat pants. (I was on to that one.) By this time in the game the arena was packed and rocking. The crowd was using this lowly "B" game as a warm-up for the real thing. They roared with every basket.

I felt cold kneeling at the scorer's table waiting to go in. But my heart was afire with the desire for personal glory and the destruction of evil.

Since this is a letter on public failure, Nate, I hardly need to tell you what happened. I'll make it short. I came in after they had scored a basket. The ball was thrown in to me, and I dribbled it up court. As I approached the top of the key I was mulling over what play to call, trying to determine exactly what form my brilliance should take.

Two things then occurred simultaneously. I heard a groan go up from our side of the gymnasium and I realized that although my hand was still going up and down, there was no ball under it.

I jerked quickly around and watched the back of the guy who had been guarding me as he glided smoothly away with the ball. I chased him futilely down the court, the groans of our fans ringing in my ears, and watched him lay the ball up for a basket.

Was I, as the Sunday-school song says, downhearted? No! No! No! (I was too stupid.) As the ball came down through the net I wasn't discouraged, I was angry. My moment of glory had merely been postponed.

A teammate grabbed the ball and threw it in-bounds to me. The other team, despite a huge lead, was pressing us full court (cross-town rivals are like that). I knew immediately that I would dribble through them the length of the court and make a driving lay-up at the other end. They would feel the full force of my wrath.

Instead, I immediately bounced the ball off my foot, and fell down at the same time. It rolled directly to one of the opponents who laid it in for another basket. Through the roar (laughter?) of the crowd pierced the nasal blast of the substitution horn. Laying on the floor, I glanced to the bench. Mr. Dee was standing with legs spread, hands on his hips, immaculate in his three-piece suit, a look of resigned exasperation on his face.

Whether my replacement came in with similar illusions I don't know. I spent the remaining few minutes of the game with a towel over my head. If I couldn't see all those people, maybe they weren't there. It didn't work, of course. Almost everyone I knew was sitting in those stands.

But something strange happened. After our game we showered, and I had to go out and sit in the stands to watch the varsity game. I had to go out and see the people who had just seen me. And you know what? My friends were still my friends. Oh, they laughed and joked and slapped me on the back. But they had a look in their eye that said, "That was awful, but we like you anyway. In fact, we like you exactly because awful things like that happen to you from time to time."

That's what friends are for—to like you when there is no advantage in it. Anybody will like you, for a while, when you score the winning basket or give a great performance in the play or otherwise carry the day. But friends are for when you are awful. Friends forgive us for being human—and that makes it easier for us to forgive ourselves.

Because you see, awful things, embarrassing things *do* happen to all of us. There is often a gap between how we would like to be and how we are, and between how we want things to go and how they sometimes do.

And that's part of what makes life interesting, Nate. If there is no chance that the ball will be stolen from you, then there is also no thrill in making a basket. It is the uncertainty in life, the possibility for things going wrong, that makes our accomplishments feel good.

And I did make a few baskets in my day, including some lucky ones. I'll tell you about a couple of those another time.

Love, Papa

SIX

=====

Mindwork, Not Schoolwork

=====

Papa, how come we have
to do so much work at school?
Why do we have to know
all this stuff?

Dear children,

THE SHORT ANSWER IS YOU DON'T HAVE TO. YOUR mom and I can *say* you have to. And your teachers can say you have to. But if you don't want to "know all this stuff" there really isn't much anyone can do about it. Everyone claims their "rights" these days, and one of those is the right to be stupid. A lot of people exercise that right, including smart people with a lot of education.

So, I think the question should really be more like, "Why should I *want* to do all the hard work to know all this stuff?" The answer to that takes a little longer.

Let's say the thing you wanted most in the world was a red ten-speed bicycle. You saved for it, you begged your parents for it, you cut out pictures of it and pasted them on your walls. Then finally, because of your hard work and the amazing generosity of your parents (that's us), you get this bike.

But you do a strange thing. You never ride the bike. You look at it. You occasionally clean it. Sometimes you even take it for a walk. But you push the bike instead of riding it. That wouldn't seem to make much sense, would it?

Well the same is true for this gift you've been given called your mind. It's like a red ten-speed (only much better), but many people never ride it. And a lot of the people who do get on for a ride just keep it in one gear. They stay away from hills because the pedaling is too hard.

What I'm saying, kids, is that your mind, your intelligence and imagination, is a wonderful thing—and each of you has plenty of it. But you need to use it. You need to use all the gears, to ride up steep hills so that you can have the pleasure of coasting down the other side, hair blowing in the breeze.

I remember sitting on our sofa with a comic book in my hands when I was four or five (we were living in the lemon orchard in Ventura). I wanted in the worst way to be able to read that comic book. I was tired of only being able to look at the pictures. And I remember saying to myself as I stared at those letters that made no sense to me, "Someday I'm going to *read* you." It was like I was giving a warning: "Watch out, alphabet, here I come!"

For me the whole universe is now like that comic book. I want to be able to read it all. I want to understand. I want to see all the beauty and truth and goodness and pain there is to see in the world. I don't want to spend the only life I have watching television.

But I can't see and understand if I don't make my mind work. Just like I can't run if I don't work my legs. And all this "stuff they make you do" at school is designed (or should be anyway) to exercise your mind. Sometimes the actual thing you are learning isn't as important as that your brain is being made to work, maybe in a new kind of way.

At times teachers are just trying to get you out of first gear into second, then out of second into third. That can be done through writing a poem or solving a math problem or discussing your thoughts about a certain idea. You may think the actual thing you're working on isn't very important or much fun, but it is part of the long process of getting into tenth gear.

When we lived with the retarded, just after Matthew was born, we saw people whose minds had been damaged. I can remember how hard some of them struggled to learn how to count change or tell time. And how what they had learned one day with great effort was often gone the next. That didn't keep many of them from being wonderful people who are gifted in many ways. But it does remind me how lucky you and I are to have minds that work pretty well. If we pushed ourselves half as hard as some of them, we could do wonders.

God has given each of you a fair share of native intelligence. When God gives you something, he expects you to use it. Fortunately, a mind is a pleasure to use. With it you can explore and create and know and feel and wonder. You can even change the world you are trying to understand. Because you are here, with your mind, doing the things you are going to do, the world is a different place. Use your mind well and it will also be a better place.

Love, Papa

SEVEN

What's Right and Wrong

My teacher says everyone
decides for themselves
about what's right and wrong.
Is that true, Papa?

Dear Matthew,

IT DEPENDS ON WHAT YOUR TEACHER MEANT. IT IS true that each of us makes decisions about what we think is right and wrong. If that's what your teacher meant, then she's right.

But if your teacher meant there is really no such thing as right and wrong, and therefore we all can just believe whatever we want, and there is no way of saying one person's belief is better than another's—then she is wrong.

A lot of people in our world today say they believe that no one can say what is right or wrong, and that we all must decide for ourselves. They say that, but they don't really believe it. And you can tell they don't believe it by watching how they act in parking lots or on tennis courts or in the bathroom.

If they are waiting in a crowded parking lot for a car to pull out so they can park, and someone else comes around them and pulls into that spot they were waiting for, they will get very angry. They will probably honk their horn, yell out the window, maybe even get out ready to fight.

Why? Because they think that person has done something wrong. And they expect that other person to *know* they have done something wrong. Would they be satisfied if that other person were to say, "In my belief system, I don't think it is wrong to take a parking place that someone else is waiting for"? You can bet your boots they would not be satisfied. In fact they would be all the madder.

Or imagine that person (who says he believes there is no way of saying what is right and wrong) playing tennis with someone. If the person he is playing against keeps saying the ball is out when it is clearly in, how will he respond? Will he say to himself, "What an interesting value system this fellow has developed. He seems to think it is right to make false statements about where my shots are landing. I respect him for that"? Are you kidding?

More likely he will think, "This guy is a *cheater!*" And he'll be right, even though calling someone else a cheater violates his own supposed belief that we all decide for ourselves what is right and wrong.

The truth is, Matthew, that there are moral laws in the universe just as there are physical laws. Moral is the word we use when we are talking about what is right and wrong. A law is a statement of how things are. The law of gravity tells you how things are in terms of objects in space. On earth, if you step off a cliff you will fall. No one has to *make* you fall. You simply *fall*—because gravity is one of the physical facts of the universe.

The same is true for moral laws. They are there. There is right and there is wrong. People talk about breaking a law. In one sense, you never really *break* a law—the law stays the same no matter what you do. What you can do is break yourself by ignoring the fact of that law. If you step off a cliff, the law of gravity is not broken, but you may be. Likewise, if you do what is wrong, the moral law is not wiped out, but you have brought on yourself the consequences of not observing the law.

Let's say you are tired of arithmetic. You have learned to count, and then to add and subtract, and then to multiply. And now, believe it or not, they want you to learn to divide. You think counting, adding, subtracting and multiplying is enough. Who needs to divide?

But you also know you will be tested on division, and you do need to pass so that you aren't still in the third grade when you are eighteen. So you come up with a plan. You will cheat on the test. How you cheat isn't important here. Somehow you figure out a way to pass the test and to pass third grade without having to learn how to divide.

Let's say you get away with it. The teacher doesn't catch you, you do pass third grade, and you didn't even have to work at division. You are the winner, right? You broke a moral law and there were no bad consequences.

But you know that isn't so, don't you? You know that there are plenty of consequences, some that are apparent right away and some that won't be apparent until later. You know you would feel a little different about yourself, and you wouldn't want your parents to find out. You know that you would be a little uncomfortable when a friend asked how you did on the test. You know that it might make you want to avoid God for a while. And you also know that someday, somewhere, someone will expect you to know how to divide. And when that day comes you won't feel very smart anymore about cheating on the test.

No one would have to punish you for having cheated. Cheating punishes itself. By cheating you would have stepped off a small cliff. If you were silly enough to think you got away with it, then there would be bigger cliffs waiting for you later.

So why are people so eager to say there is no right and wrong that is true for everybody? One reason is that it is not always easy to say what is right and wrong in every situation. Cheating is a pretty easy one, but others are tougher. Up-to-date relativists like to ask whether it's okay for a poor person to steal an expensive medicine to save his dying daughter. And because situations are often difficult, some people find it easier just to give up. They shrug their shoulders with a "Who's to say?" (Don't try taking their parking places though.)

To me, that would be like a scientist who was trying to find the answer to a tough problem saying, "Well, this is really complex. There are lots of different possible explanations. I guess none of them is any truer than any other. It's whatever you think." Scientists don't work that way. They believe that in the great majority of cases there is an answer to a problem, and that one answer is better than the others.

So if a problem of what is right and wrong is difficult, then we have to work hard to find the right answer. And we may disagree with each other sometimes. But that doesn't mean there is no right and wrong. It only means we are not perfect and often don't fully understand how things really are.

And things *are* the way God made them. He made the physical world and we understand it in part by seeking the laws that reveal it. And God also made the spiritual world (which might not be as separate from the physical one as we think), and that world is revealed through his moral laws.

And God gave us ways of knowing what these laws are so that we might live by them if we so choose. He gave us minds that can think, and imaginations that penetrate and create, and he gave us the Bible through which he speaks with us. And most important, he gave us Jesus Christ so that we could see the beauty of a life lived in perfect harmony with how things really are, and through seeing that, want such a life for ourselves.

But this *is* a choice. And if your teacher meant that we all have to decide whether to choose the truth or to reject it, then she is right. My greatest hope for you is that you will choose well.

Love, Papa

EIGHT

Thinking about God

Papa, what did you think
about God when you
were a kid? Did you
always believe in him?

D ear children,

YOU ASK THIS QUESTION THE WAY YOU DO BECAUSE
we have attended a Presbyterian church most of your lives. If you
had been raised in Baptist churches like I was, you would ask it
the good old-fashioned way: "Papa, when were you saved?"

The short answer is, "I don't know." Maybe it was when I was
five years old, sitting in an evening service somewhere in an
unfamiliar southern church, listening to my father preach. I
don't remember what he said, but I do remember realizing that
I was a sinner. I knew I was not only capable of doing wrong,
but that I actually chose to do it at times. And I knew that was
no small thing.

After the service, my dad came down to where we three boys
were sitting in the second row. He talked to us and I cried and
he prayed for us. Afterward, I felt better. Maybe I was "saved"
then.

Or maybe it was when I was nine years old. We lived in a little
town in the panhandle of Texas called Wheeler. Wheeler had

eleven-hundred people living in it, bigger than the other towns around because it was the county seat.

Grandpa Darrell was the pastor of the Southern Baptist church. (You can't get any more Baptist than that.) Again it was a Sunday night and again I don't remember what he preached about.

But I do remember feeling this heavy weight on my heart. I visualized it as a brick. I felt I was distant from God and I needed to do something about it. In Baptist churches they give you lots of opportunities for taking care of such things. They call them invitations. You are invited to "come forward," to walk down the aisle of the church and shake the preacher's hand, to tell him and God whatever is on your mind and heart.

Some Christians think this is kind of hokey, but I think there's a lot to be said for it. I remember standing there that night as we sang the closing hymn. (They always sing a hymn to give the other people something to do while you are feeling rotten and making up excuses why you don't need to go forward.)

I remember agonizing through the first two verses. (A good Baptist preacher gives a four-verse altar-call because he knows Satan can keep anyone in his seat for at least two verses, but only a real tough case can hold out for four.) I wanted more than anything to get rid of this brick on my heart, but the last thing I wanted was to have everybody look at me as I walked down the aisle.

I think I gave in somewhere in the third verse. The first step was like walking in deep mud with concrete shoes, but the second step was light as a feather. I felt the brick break away. I remember your grandpa having tears in his eyes as I shook his hand. After the service I went down the church steps by threes.

Maybe that was when I was saved.

But I don't think so. I don't think I was saved at any one

moment. I think I was blessed by being raised in a home where God was both taken for granted and wasn't. That is, it was taken for granted that God was who the Bible said he was, but it wasn't assumed that God would be happy with us no matter how we lived our lives.

There were expectations. We didn't have a lot of detailed rules because we didn't need them. Some of the expectations might have been a little peculiar, but pity the child for whom there are none.

God became a part of my daily life. It's not that I prayed a lot or read the Bible much, but somehow he was around. He was around when I was tempted to cheat on my spelling tests (once I cheated anyway). He was around when I started thinking there were monsters in my bedroom who would bite off any part of me sticking out from under the covers. He was around when I tried to figure out why Debbie died of leukemia.

Later, I began asking a lot of questions of God, sometimes hard, accusing questions. I wondered at times whether he was even there at all. I considered other ways of explaining the world that left God out. And that was okay—he was around then too.

Of course, God wants to be more than just "around." He wants to talk with you through your mind and heart (and maybe, who knows, even through your ears!). He wants you to know he loves you and he forgives you and that he wants to teach you how to live.

That, I think, is what it means to be saved. It means working God into the rhythm of your daily life. It means your life being different than it otherwise would be. I think my life has been. My greatest hope is that the same will be true for you Matthew, and you Julie, and you Nate.

Love, Papa

NINE

Being Afraid

Papa, I'm afraid of having
bad dreams tonight.
Have you ever been afraid?

Dear Nate,

OF COURSE NOT. I'M A MAN, SEE, AND MEN AREN'T ever . . . that is, men almost never . . . which is to say, yes, I have been afraid many times.

I think people are afraid of different things in different ways at different times of their lives. When I was a child I was, like most children, afraid of things that go *bump* in the night. I remember when I was about seven playing this game in my mind as I lay in bed at night. It would be dark and I would stare at the black, coiled springs of the top bunk where my brother lay. Something about those springs, spirals within rectangles in the shadowy darkness of a Texas night, suggested other, fearful worlds. They made me wonder about what lived under the springs of my own mattress on the bottom bunk.

But I told myself (for no good reason) that monsters which lie under beds cannot break through blankets and sheets! Furthermore (also for no good reason), I told myself that they weren't interested in children's heads—only in their legs and hands and arms. So, I reasoned, as long as I kept my hands and feet inside the blanket and kept it tucked tightly under my chin, I would be safe from the worst that any under-the-bed creature could do. It didn't always make for comfort on a hot, Panhandle night, but it kept the fear in check.

Looking back on it now, I think I was also afraid of one other thing as a child. I was afraid of censure—of getting in trouble. I didn't want people to be mad at me. I almost cried in sixth grade when the principal told us boys we had to quit skipping lunch so that we could get to the baseball diamond first—and he wasn't even angry. I think you're a little that way too, Nate.

By the time I was a teen-ager I wasn't afraid of what might live under my bed, but I was afraid of what my friends might have to say about the way I combed my hair. (I had a lot of it then.) I can remember my first day of junior high school. I was sitting in our bedroom getting dressed when my older brother (Uncle Steve), far wiser in the ways of the world, gasped with astonishment. "You're not going to wear buckets to junior high, are you?" he said. I looked down at the bottoms of my brand-new jeans, with cuffs rolled stiffly up four or five inches.

"Why not?" I said with cautious defiance. I had worn my jeans this way all through grade school and had been widely thought a wonderful fellow. Why should I change for junior high? I went to school determined to defend the honor of buckets no matter what the cost. On the way to my first-period class, having seen nary a bucket anywhere, I quietly crouched down and tucked the extra material up inside my pant leg, never to wear buckets again. I didn't recognize that as an act of fear at the time, but I see now that it was.

Throughout junior high and high school I feared somewhat the ridicule of friends. My friends were good friends, the kind you want to have, but we were prone to petty cruelty just like lots of teen-agers are. The trick in our group was to keep the focus of attention off yourself. Someone was going to get his ego handed to him in a plastic bag; you just didn't want it to be yours more often than necessary. If today I am somewhat impervious to the disapproval of others, it is perhaps because I've suffered it at the hands of masters.

What do I fear now? Not bumps in the night, not the opinion of others, not disapproval or getting in trouble. I am tempted to say that I am not genuinely fearful about anything—but that isn't true. My main fear now is insignificance. I am afraid, to put it simply, of living a life that doesn't matter. I am afraid of leaving the world exactly as I found it, no different for my having been here. I am afraid, as the writer Henry Thoreau said, of coming to the end of life and finding that I have not lived.

A lot of people say something like that these days, but they think "having lived" means having a lot of adventures or a lot of fun or a lot of money. I don't think that has much to do with it. Significant living comes from filling your life with things which last forever. That's why the usual things people seek to guarantee importance in their lives—money, fame, power— don't work very well. They all come to an end, often during the person's own life, and certainly thereafter.

What are things which last forever? Justice, mercy, forgiveness, compassion and grace are a few. Truth also lasts forever. These are all forms of the greatest value of all—love. And as you know, Nate, the source and perfect giver of love is God.

If I want my life to count, to be significant, then I will try to fill it as much as possible with these attitudes and actions. I may do all kinds of specific things with my life, but they will only be important if they are enveloped in the things which always last. If you have made someone else's life better, you have done something eternal. And that means that a significant life will usually have lots of people in it. Because people are the only part of this world which last forever.

And it occurs to me, Nate, that you and Matthew and Julie are my best evidence that I do not need to fear an insignificant life. In bringing you all into the world, your mother and I have made it a better place. Through us God has continued his creativity, his ongoing blessing of the world he has made.

All these fears, those of my childhood and those of my present, have something in common. They are the result of insecurity. If there might be a monster under my bed, I do not feel safe. If the principal yells at me, I do not feel safe. If my friends ridicule me, I do not feel safe. If my life has no significance, I do not feel safe.

This world is filled with threats—some imagined, some real—to our safety, to our sense of being okay. The ultimate security, the only true safety, is to be in right relationship with the God who is the alpha and omega, the beginning and the end. He was there before the beginning. He has no end. He has seen and suffered all. He has known our fears. He sets us free.

Give God your fears, Nate. It won't always keep your heart from beating fast or your stomach from churning, but it can give you a sense of peace at the deepest level which goes far beyond human understanding.

Love, Papa

TEN

Bored by Church

Church is getting boring.
Why do we have to
go to church?

Dear Matthew,

I COULD TELL YOU STORIES ABOUT CHURCH FROM NOW to the Second Coming. I went to so much church as a kid that wearing all my attendance pins at once would have made me look like a Russian general. I went to four services on Sunday, one on Wednesday, and wedged in a youth group activity or two in between. I know about church!

And I know that you are right—sometimes it can be boring. I used to sleep a lot in church. When you're little that's okay. You try to beat your brother or sister to your mother's lap, stretch your legs out on the pew (if your mom will let you) and enjoy the lulling rise and fall of voices as you drift in and out of sleep. Nothing could be better.

But when you get a little older, you're too big to lay down and go to sleep, but not big enough to follow totally what the preacher is talking about (even if he *is* your dad). You can quietly (that's a joke) tear open the offering envelopes and draw, but that usually only gets you through the song service. You burn out on drawing about the time the preacher starts heading for point number one of his sermon.

I remember one Sunday evening service. I must have been about eight or nine. I was sitting by myself right on the aisle in the very front pew—right under Grandpa Darrell's nose. A word of advice—don't sit there, especially on a Sunday night.

I got very sleepy, but I was too big and too conspicuously placed to lay down. I tried desperately to fight it off. No way. I dropped off to sleep. And as I did my neck relaxed and my head fell back and knocked loudly against the wooden pew. It sounded like a cannon shot inside my head. I startled awake, sure that everyone in the church had heard it and was staring at the preacher's kid sawing logs in the front row.

Fear kept me wide awake—for about two minutes. Then I would fall asleep again, and my head would boom against the pew again, and I would awake with a start again. And so it went through what seemed the longest sermon ever preached in the long annals of long Baptist sermons.

So I know church doesn't always seem like an exciting place. But let me tell you part of why I think we should go, whether it seems exciting or not. When God made us, he made us so that we get hungry. He did that, I think, so that we would want to seek after the things which would satisfy that hunger. Because he knew that there was something good in looking and working for things, as well as in actually having them.

One thing we hunger for, of course, is food. (And if you go to the right kind of church you can get loads of it. Sometime I'll tell you about those wonderful potluck socials.) But God also gave us a hunger for being with other human beings. And he gave us a tremendous hunger for himself. He wants us to want him and to want to be with other people.

The church is God's way of satisfying all these hungers at

once. It is in the church that we come to meet each other, to see and talk and touch, to comfort ourselves that there are others who are hungry like us.

And it is in the church that all of us together unite to satisfy our hunger for God. Of course we can and must know God by ourselves, but God wants us to come together to know even more. It's like each of us holds a little candle that is part of the light of God. When we get together the many lights join, and we can see and feel more of what God is.

This happens not because people who go to church are such good people. Anybody who has spent much time in church knows they aren't. It happens because God said it would. He told us that wherever there are two or three people together who believe in him, then he will be there. And what could be better than being where God is?

Think about it. If a friend of yours called and said that a famous athlete or singer or actor was going to be at his house, and asked if you wanted to come over, wouldn't you go? And wouldn't you be excited? Of course! And so would I.

Well, church is the place where God will be, every time you go. Of course he is with you whether you're in church or not, but he can be there in a special and powerful way when many believers gather to celebrate him together.

"Sounds great," I hear you saying, "but then how come you fell asleep so much? If God is really there, I mean *really* there, then how come we aren't bug-eyed and breathless most all the time?"

That's a very good question. I wish I had a very good answer. Part of it is that God knows we can't take very much of him. It's like when you hold Fluffs, our hamster. If you squeezed very hard, Fluffs would be on his way to hamster heaven. You have to hold him gently, talk to him quietly. Well, God has to be sort of like that with us.

Truthfully, though, the biggest reason might be that we don't want very much of God. We want God to stay in his cage like Fluffs does. We are afraid of losing control of our own lives. We just want him to help us a little here, and forgive us a little there, and let us handle the rest. And so we try to make church a safe place where we can get a little bit of God but not too much.

We don't like surprises, not even from God, so we make our churches places where surprises aren't likely to happen. We ask God to come, but only if he will be polite. And therefore, little kids and adult kids often fall asleep—even if they keep their eyes open.

In many ways the church is something of a sorry place. It's only rarely what it could be. There's always this gap between what it is and what it knows it should be, just like you and I don't always do as well as we could.

And yet, at the very same time, church is a wonderful place. God has chosen it, sorriness and all, to be the place where he will meet his people, the place from which he will send his people to all parts of the world to preach the good news about him. For two thousand years, and for two thousand years before that, God has said, "If you love me, gather together and I will come among you and I will fill you with power. I will be your God and you will be my people." And the church has always been sort of a comical place where we never get it exactly right for long. And yet all of our weakness, timidity and love of ruts does not lessen the centrality of the church or God's ability to use it to do what he wants done in the world—which is plenty.

So, Matthew, our family goes to church because we expect to meet God there in a way that is different from how we meet him in our own individual lives. We go there to tell God, as best we can, how much we love him. We go there to be encouraged and healed. We go there to find out what God wants *us* to do in his world, and to get the power to do it.

There's a feeling you get sometimes in church. It happens occasionally even during the boring times. It happens when you are among others who want to know God and you are singing a song or hearing God's Word. It's a feeling that says, "This is what life is about. Other things are not very important. Knowing and worshiping and serving God is." That feeling, which involves your mind as well as your heart, explains better than any words why we go to church.

It's too bad that church often seems boring; it shouldn't be that way. But don't give up. God has promised to be there, and he's kept his promise for thousands of years. If you look you will find him there, and then you'll understand what church is all about.

Love, Papa

ELEVEN

Giving
Money

My Sunday school teacher says
we should give ten per cent
of our money to the church.
How come? Does God
really need our money?

Dear Julie,

NO, GOD DOESN'T NEED OUR MONEY. SOMEONE WHO created the Milky Way can get along fine without our quarters. God doesn't even need money, as we are often told, "to do his work." (People who *proclaim* God often can't do what *they* want to do because of low funds, but that's another question.)

Can you imagine God being kept from doing what he wills to do because he's a little short on cash? If that's the case, maybe the church should check into getting him a credit card. Maybe a platinum one to give him a little feeling of prestige, with the word "God" stamped on it. (I wonder if they would make him show his license for identification?)

If we are expected by Scripture to give money to the church, my guess is it's for our benefit, not for God's. The ten per cent comes from the Old Testament where the Jews are told to give one tenth of their crops and the like to the Temple. Some people say the tithe, as it's called, doesn't apply to Christians of our time. They may be right. Based on how much money the average

North American Christian makes, one tenth is probably way too low.

This giving-money-to-God business has its pros and cons. Your mother remembers sitting in church when she was four or five. She had this little blue plastic purse that she liked very much, and it had all the money she commanded, probably a few nickels, a dime or two and maybe a quarter. The minister was preaching on "the widow's mite." That's a story Jesus told about a very poor woman giving all she had to the synagogue, even though it was almost nothing, and how her gift was better than the much bigger gifts of the rich, who gave only a small portion of all they had.

Your mom, even at her young age (she's *still* quite young of course), was able to understand what Jesus and the minister were talking about. When the velvet offering pouch with the two handles came around (they were Lutherans), she opened up her little blue plastic purse and turned it upside down, dumping all her coins into the pouch. She looked up at her parents, and they smiled proudly down at her, covering her in the kind of beaming affirmation that little kids crave. She's been a giver ever since.

I, on the other hand, had a more ambivalent experience in my first attempt at tithing. I was eight or nine years old and the proud amasser of a ten-dollar fortune. I didn't know exactly what you could or couldn't buy for ten dollars, but my hunch was that if I was careful it would buy pretty much everything I needed for the rest of my life.

Then I heard about tithing. I'm sure I had heard of it before, but this time I heard about it in the way that points a great big finger at you and makes you feel funny inside until you've taken care of things. So one Sunday morning I got out my hoard and picked out a dollar bill. It was the first time I had given money you could fold, and it felt like an awesome thing to do.

At church, I watched that offering plate coming closer and closer, silently passed from row to row by the plumbers-turned-ushers who looked slightly uncomfortable in their Sunday suits. Out of the corner of my eye I watched the plate glide down our pew toward me, the boy who was going to give a dollar, the tithing boy. And I put the dollar in quickly but solemnly, certain that God and all the angels of heaven were watching with approval—"This is Danny Taylor, in whom I am well pleased!"

I felt great about it, just like your mother did when she emptied her blue plastic wallet. I felt that with my dollar there was no telling what God could do now. Maybe even turn those dreaded Russians into Christians.

That feeling lasted until the following Sunday morning. While getting dressed for church, somewhere between polishing my miniature black wingtips and putting on my already tied tie, it occurred to me that they would be taking the offering again today. Those same plumber ushers would be silently passing the plates down those same rows—because there were no days off in God's work and that required continued, even continuous, giving on the part of his people.

It was obvious that if you had to tithe one Sunday, you also had to tithe the next. So I drug out my glass jar, confirmed that I nine dollars left, and faithfully, but not enthusiastically, counted out ninety cents.

The third week I started feeling rebellious. Not only was it getting harder to figure out what I owed, but it was clear that in the not-too-distant future I wouldn't have anything *left* to give. God was asking for too much!

As it turns out, I had made a mistake. I wasn't expected to give ten per cent every week on the same sum of money, only on new money that might come my way. But my attitude, mistaken or not, was typical and revealing.

I got a lot of satisfaction out of giving that first dollar, and figured God must have been pretty pleased that I had chosen to believe in him. I gave the second tithe more reluctantly, but figured that pain and martyrdom came with the territory if one was going to be a Christian. In the third week, however, I decided that *other* people could audition for sainthood; I was going to keep what I had left for baseball cards.

Most religious people are like me. They'll give the first buck freely, but watch out if you mess with their baseball card money. Either openly or secretly, when confronted with the expectation that we part with some of our money, we have the basic human-being-shopping-mall response: *what's in it for me?* I think it's a fair question, and one to which there are a variety of popular answers at the moment.

One of the most common is the old line, "You can't outgive God." This says, "Don't worry about giving your money to the church because you will get it all back and plenty more." It's kind of an E. F. Hutton approach to giving. You invest in God and his work and you'll get a big return on your investment (God having had an excellent return-on-investment record over the last ten thousand years or so).

This is fine unless you assume the payback always is, or should be, in money. Then it's baloney at the best, and a very foolish heresy at the worst. A man in Florida sued a pastor who made claims like this because after a year he couldn't see that he'd gotten any of his money back, much less made a profit. Based on what he'd been told, he had a beef. Unfortunately, he'd been told wrong. Christians who succumb to society's equation of success and blessing with material prosperity testify not to the "good news" but to the poverty of their own spiritual imaginations.

Another common answer to "what's in it for me?" is that it

will make you feel good—about yourself. This is what your mom felt when her parents smiled at her, and it's okay as far as it goes. It doesn't explain *why* giving something away makes you feel good, or why feeling good is a good thing, but it's certainly better than the return-on-investment approach.

A third answer, one that attracts me a bit more than these other two, is the "it's not yours in the first place" answer. This says that we have reversed the question. It shouldn't be, "How much of my money should I give to God (and why)?" but rather, "How much of God's money am I going to keep for myself (and why)?"

This gives a different feel to the question. It assumes that God is the source of all good things, including material things. We may think it's ours because *we* have worked so hard for it, but that ignores who gave us life for working, work to do, and the physical and mental skills to do it—all of which can disappear at any time. It would be like you borrowing a bicycle from your friend, riding it around all day, and then coming back and charging your friend for the effort you went to in riding his bike.

So if the question becomes how much of this money that God has made available to us do we intend to spend solely on ourselves, then giving God back ten per cent doesn't look overly generous. Scrooge, by comparison, looks like Santa Claus.

I think there's something to this third answer, and to all the answers if properly qualified, but somehow none of them satisfies me. And I don't know that I have a better one.

Maybe it has something to do with the way we are made. We should give for the same reason that we should exercise our bodies. Our muscles are made so that they are best off when forced to work. If you "save" your muscles by never making them do anything, you actually are hurting them and yourself. You haven't "spent" any energy, but, strangely, the result is you have less strength and energy than if you had. Eventually you become like a jellyfish plopped helplessly on the beach.

Something like this is true of your giving muscles as well. God has made us to be givers. It isn't something we *have* to do in order to please him so much as it's something we need to do to keep ourselves working properly. We are healthy and whole when we are both giving and receiving.

When your mother breast-fed you as babies, she had lots of milk to give. If she didn't give it, it was bad for you, but it was also painful for her. She needed to give you the milk almost as much as you needed to take it. Giving you that milk was part of what it meant for her to be a mother. And giving is also part of what it means for us to be human beings.

Giving money is only one kind of giving, and not the most important. Time is in shorter supply for most people than money, and many are more stingy with it even than with their dollars—including with their own families.

Giving is really more an attitude toward life than it is a specific act at one time or another. Giving people offer friendship easily; they are openhanded not only with their money but with emotions. They are quick to encourage and console. They take genuine delight in the good fortune of others. They think of strangers only as people who they haven't happened yet to meet.

Givers have a certain openness about them. They are not aggressively competitive. They do not speak a lot about their "rights." They generally laugh a lot and have very little self-pity. They do not run constant cost-benefit analyses to see if an opportunity for generosity is to their advantage. They are not attached like lampreys to the things in their lives.

As it happens, giving is to your benefit. It doesn't make you a saint or martyr to give. In giving you are simply reflecting God's image—he who gave everything. Miserliness in all forms—monetary and emotional—diminishes us. The more we keep the less we have. And the less we are.

This is one of life's interesting paradoxes.

Love, Papa

TWELVE

Why Pray?

Papa, how come when I pray
for something it sometimes
doesn't work? And why pray at all
if God already knows everything
that is going to happen?

Dear Julie,

SOMETHING SEEMS A LITTLE STRANGE HERE, DOESN'T it? We are told to pray and that prayer works; we are told that God honors prayer; and yet sometimes it seems that we pray for something that even God should want —like somebody we love getting healed or a friend discovering God—and yet it doesn't happen.

I remember struggling real hard with this when I was eleven and twelve. I loved the Dodgers. I couldn't see how anyone could help but love the Dodgers. Nothing made me happier than having the Dodgers win. Nothing made be sadder than when they lost.

I used to pray a lot for the Dodgers. I prayed that they would win and that each of the players would be a good person so that God would want them to win. But deep in my heart I knew that the real key to their winning was for *me* to be a good person.

I had it figured this way. I was a Christian. I believed in God, and he liked that. He also liked that I prayed for the Dodgers, even though the truth was I usually only started praying in the eighth inning of close games. I don't know whether I was afraid to "use up" God's blessing by wasting it on blowouts or whether I thought the Dodgers could win some games on their own without me and God helping.

Anyway, I had it figured that praying was the right thing to do, but that God was only going to give me what I prayed for if I deserved it. That meant things like not cheating in school (which was usually easy to obey) and letting my brother have the biggest piece of cake even when I was there first (which was a lot harder).

This was a great moral responsibility. Sandy Koufax might never have learned to control his fast ball if I hadn't learned to control my love of chocolate cake. But at least it was simple in theory. Do good and your prayers will be answered; don't and they won't.

Then one day it dawned on me that I wasn't the only one praying during the late innings of these games. While I was praying for Koufax to strike out Willie Mays, some other Christian kid was praying that Mays would hit a home run. This was a real theological dilemma. How did God know what to do? Two kids, both devout, both trying to be good, praying for opposite things at the same time.

After some struggle, I decided it was purely a matter of arithmetic. God took all the goodness of all the people who were praying for Mays to strike out, and weighed it against all the goodness of all the people who were praying for Mays to get a home run. Whosoever goodness weighed the most got their prayers answered, and the others didn't and that was only fair. (Later I started to worry about whether it was fair that there were potentially many more Christians in Los Angeles to accumulate goodness for the Dodgers than there were in San

Francisco, but I won't get into that.)

Looking back now, I see that I didn't understand much about prayer. And in many ways I still don't. But I do know more now about what prayer is not.

First off, prayer isn't a "deal" with God. It isn't a matter of a contract where you perform on your end and God has to do something he agreed to. And it isn't magic words, where if we say the right words in the right way God is forced into action.

And more than anything, prayer isn't (like I thought when I prayed for the Dodgers) a case where we earn the right for our prayers to be answered. We need to talk to God most, perhaps, when we deserve it least.

Okay, what is it then? Let me start by saying you really should speak to your mom about this. She knows a lot more than I do because she has spent more time on her knees. But I'll tell you what I think I know.

God made us to talk. We don't always have to use words, but we do have to communicate. We aren't fully human beings in God's image unless we do. Humans have been talking ever since we were created.

We talk for lots of reasons and in lots of different ways. Every time we paint a painting we are talking, or write a poem or sing a song or send a letter or wave to a friend. One of the reasons we talk is to make certain that we are not alone. Think how frightening it would be to find you were the only person alive in the whole universe. No one else. Not one. Just you.

And many are afraid this might be the case even though they see people all around them. Because if they can't talk one way or another, if they can't communicate something of what they think and feel, then they are alone, trapped inside their own heads.

So God wants all of us to be able to talk, even those with no voices. He wants us to talk to each other—through friendship, art, marriage, the church and so on. But, perhaps even more, he wants us to talk to him. Some people think God needs for us to talk to him. (Others say God doesn't need anything, but I'm not sure that's as complimentary to God as they think it is.)

Whether God needs to talk to us or not, he certainly desires to, and we certainly need to talk to him. And that is what prayer is for. It's the main way we talk to God. (Painting a picture is sometimes another way.)

What does God want to talk about? The same things we do, really. He wants to hear how our day has been. (Even though he knows, he likes to hear it from us in our own words.) He wants us to tell him where we haven't done the things we know we should have done and to ask him to not hold that against us because we are sorry. And he won't.

He wants us to tell him that we love him, and that we appreciate all the things he has done for us. He likes hearing these things. It gives him pleasure. And he deserves some pleasure. He also wants us to tell him what we hope for, what it seems to us would be good, how things should be as far as we can tell. That might include the Dodgers beating the Giants or Uncle Clinton and Mr. Cuendet getting well or your friend's dad getting a job or another friend's parents not getting divorced or you doing well on your spelling test.

And this is where things get complicated. How does God decide what to do when we ask him for something? Does it really do any good to ask? Isn't he going to do whatever he wants anyway?

The short answer is, we don't know—or at least I don't. God didn't tell us how these things work. But he has told us one very important thing—we *are* supposed to pray. He says it *does* matter. He says, "Tell me what you want, how you feel. I want to know.

I want to hear it from you. It matters to me."

And if God says to do something, it has always been my experience that the best thing is to do it. I have a guess as to why maybe God hasn't told us how this works. (This is only a guess.) I think maybe if we knew how it worked we would stop *talking*. If we thought we had it worked out how prayer got answered, we would keep asking, even demanding, but would stop really talking. We'd put in our orders, you might say, and not really talk with the One who made us. We do that quite a bit even as it is.

So why when we prayed for Mr. Cuendet did he get well, but when we prayed for Uncle Clinton, God took him to heaven instead? I don't know. God never promised to tell me why everything happens the way it does. But he did promise me that anytime I wanted to talk, he would be happy to listen. And in a world where so many people feel they are all alone, that's a pretty great thing to know.

One more thing. God not only listens, he talks too. So when you are praying, *keep your ears open!*

Love, Papa

THIRTEEN

Fighting Back

Papa, if someone is being mean
or something, is it okay
to slug him? Were you ever in
any fights when you were a kid?

Dear Nate,

I HAVE TWO ANSWERS. ONE IS MY "I KNOW I OUGHT to say" answer, and the other is my "Just between you and me" answer.

I'll start with the second one first. Sometimes it feels awfully good to contemplate punching a jerk in the nose. Whether it's right or wrong is another question, but the idea *feels* great. That assumes, of course, that the jerk doesn't turn around and knock your teeth out. In the movies that rarely happens, but in real life it's a distinct possibility.

Yes, I had some fights when I was a kid. Mostly that meant I wrestled some guy down and sat on him. It wasn't what you'd call heavy-duty martial-arts stuff. You'd get the guy down, sit on his stomach, pin his arms to the ground by holding his wrists (and putting your knees on his biceps if he was a really tough customer), and then asking with a certain air of invincibility, "Do you give?"

If he said, "No," then you sat on him a while longer until he faced the inevitable.

Maybe one reason I got in more than my share of fights was that I was always the new kid. When you are the new kid, you often have to be evaluated, especially on how tough you are. I seem to remember, however, that most of my fights were in defense of some underdog or some principle of justice. Maybe I am just being kind to myself.

When I was in third grade, I was sitting in the lunch room beside the dirtiest kid in the school. His hair was thick and tangled and filthy. His neck was so dirty it looked like you could grow potatoes on it. And he had a personality to match. He was, all liberal tenderheartedness aside, a mean kid. Everyone else was afraid of him. I was too stupid.

I don't have any recollection that on this particular day there were any bad feelings between us or even that I had spoken to him. I was simply sitting beside him eating my sandwich when I felt him staring at me and I turned my head. He had a look in his eye that I don't know how to describe except to say that it convinced me on the spot that there really was such a thing as personal evil.

Suddenly, he spewed his chewed sandwich into my face— peanut butter, jelly, spit and all. It was like peering into a garbage disposal and having everything come flying up into your face—only worse. I was too shocked to do anything except reach blindly for my napkin as he walked away.

Later, out on the playground, I don't remember if it was the same day, I found him picking on some little kids. I took up their cause, which was of course really my cause as well. I ended up sitting on his stomach, my knees on his biceps, asking him, "Do you give?" He said yes, and I felt that there was justice in the universe.

The closest I came to losing one of these "sit on their

stomach" fights was that same year. I had started third grade in Wheeler, Texas, but we had moved first to Azusa, California—where I had this fight with the dirt-necked kid—and then to Ventura, where I finished third grade. I had lived in various parts of Texas for five years and had a certain pride in being from the place most associated in the minds of these kids with cowboys and desperados and shoot-outs and the like.

I don't remember at all what this fight was about, only that there were lots of kids watching and that I was getting my butt kicked. It was a new feeling to have the other guy be stronger than I was. In short order *he* was sitting on *my* stomach asking me the fatal question, "Do you give?" I remember all these kids crowded around us, watching the new boy get his welcome to the playground. It was humiliating, but I didn't have any choice but to acknowledge defeat.

The fellow started getting off me with a look of satisfaction on his face. But as I lay there, my feet were cocked out at an angle and the kid tripped over them as he backed away, falling hard onto the seat of his pants. I immediately leaped to my feet, stared down at him with a look of nonchalant contempt and heard myself saying, *"That's* how we do it in Texas." I turned and walked through the path the crowd made for me, leaving them all to contemplate the price of messing with someone from the land of the Alamo.

My attitude toward fighting changed a lot in junior high—almost not soon enough. One day in gym class I began arguing with one of the toughest guys in our school. Steve Atlas was his name and it fit. A wiser friend of mine kept trying to get me to shut up, but I was full of righteousness and ready to engage this guy in a stomach-sitting contest if he thought he was up to it. Fortunately, the bell rang and I didn't have to learn firsthand that when boys become teen-agers they don't sit on each other's stomachs anymore.

Not long after, I saw my first real fight. The word spread in advance. "It's going to be at The Trees, after school." I went along with fifty or sixty others to see what was going to happen. It was shocking. These guys were both tough and they hated each other. They walked quickly and eagerly across the grass from opposite directions and, without a single hesitation or word, began punching each other in the face. There was no wrestling or holding, just punches and kicks and blood.

I hated it. I felt sorry for these two guys, and I didn't like being part of this crowd that yelled with every punch, encouraging the two to keep at it, to fight to the finish. I walked away, if I remember right, while the fight was still going on. I felt like I had been part of something evil.

Maybe I just wasn't very tough. After all, I was the one who used to feel sorry for the fish I caught and wanted to throw them back when no one was looking.

The last physical fight I ever had was with a friend. Larry, Chuck and I were playing basketball in Chuck's back yard. We were about eighteen. The game was a little rough, and Larry and I got into a fight. It lasted about twenty seconds and ended with Chuck sitting there laughing at both of us. Something about his laughter made it hard to keep punching.

It's too bad it doesn't work that way with countries. Countries get very serious and self-important and self-righteous when they go to war. They tell themselves the war is necessary, even inevitable, and that goodness, justice and truth demand it. That is very seldom the case, but not enough people laugh. It sounds too good not to be true.

Every generation, it seems, is offered its chance at war. My generation's war was in Vietnam. I didn't go.

Vietnam was neither the good war for the good cause that we

were originally told, nor was it the evil war of evil imperialists that a different kind of propaganda later claimed. It was a war that showed us our confusion, as a nation and as individual human beings.

It was also a war that killed some of my friends. It would be wrong to claim a great personal loss from their death. I was not close to them at the time they died. They were not my brothers or lifelong companions. But they were guys who were on my baseball teams, in my gym classes, who rode my bus, who lived down the street.

One was my best friend in sixth grade. But I had moved and hadn't seen him in six or seven years when one day I found his picture in the paper. Mike looked the same in his army helmet as he had looked on a pitcher's mound wearing a baseball cap— serious. And the caption to the picture said he was dead, killed in Vietnam, and that was all.

I didn't go into any rage against war, against fighting, against the folly of being in Vietnam or in any other war. But I did feel sad and diminished. I did wonder whether it was really necessary, much less inevitable, that Mike should die before he was twenty, so many thousands of miles away from home. I doubted greatly that it was.

Last spring I visited Mike in Washington, D. C. There is a memorial there to those who were killed in Vietnam. Their names are written, in the order in which they died, on large slabs of black stone. There are more than fifty thousand of them. Books are available to tell you where individual names are located.

In some ways I felt like I didn't deserve to be there. I didn't go to Vietnam, nor even into the army. I went to graduate school instead. I was lucky, of course, but I also missed something.

I found Mike's name—and Jerry's and Anton's and a couple

of others. And strangely, I feel their loss more now, twenty years later, than I did at the time. I have lived longer since their deaths than they were allowed to live in total—meandering, lukewarm years, but life nonetheless. And I have the reasonable prospect of twenty or thirty or forty years more.

Their lives, on the other hand, ended quickly and violently before they could even decide what life was for. I cannot say what I think about fighting without considering its cost for them.

The truth is, I'm not totally sure what I think about fighting. Perhaps there are times we need to fight and *not* to fight is evil. It has been said that if there is nothing you will die for, then you have nothing to live for. There is merit to that.

But I think we had better be very slow to fight at least. Christ told us to turn the other cheek and not to repay evil for evil. To some that sounds like weakness. I think life proves that it takes much greater strength and courage than fighting does. Christ knew, perhaps, that when we fight we tend to fight only for ourselves, and often for our worst selves.

If we fight, we should be as sure as we can that we are fighting *against evil,* that we are fighting to make the world a better place, and not fighting just for ourselves, not just because we have created an "enemy" that it will give us satisfaction to destroy. This should be true whether we are talking about physical fights or verbal ones (words can hurt more than punches), and true for our church and country as well as for us as individuals.

Fighting is usually a sign of weakness and failure. But it is sometimes necessary. God grant you the wisdom to discern the difference.

Love, Papa

FOURTEEN

Faulty Friends

Papa, why do my friends
say mean things behind each
other's backs? Do you think they
say mean things about me
when I'm not around?

Dear Julie,

IN SOME WAYS I AM SORRY THAT YOU ARE GROWING up. There is a lot of ugliness in the world and you are starting to see it.

Your friends say unkind things about each other because they are afraid. They do not feel safe in the world. Another word for this is insecurity. When you are insecure you will do anything, even the ugliest things, to try to feel safer.

What does safety have to do with saying mean things? Well, there are many ways in which people need to feel safe. One is the need for physical safety. We don't want lions to jump out of a tree on top of us or cars to hit us or disease to make us sick or robbers to hit us on the head. We want to protect our bodies.

But we also want to protect our spirits and what we are inside. People will do violent things in order to protect their bodies, but nothing approaches what they will do to protect themselves inside.

One of the ways we feel safer on the inside is if we have

friends. If we feel that other people like us and want to be with us and will help us when necessary, then we feel less afraid. Unfortunately, a lot of times we are not convinced that we are likeable, that people really will be our friends no matter what.

One way of making sure that you keep your friends is to be the best possible friend you can be. Do the things that friends do for friends. Unfortunately, there is another way, a wrong way, that we fall into without even having to think about it. That way is to try to make ourselves look like a better friend by making someone else look like a worse one.

If your friend gossips to you about another friend who isn't there, she is not only saying, "Did you hear what so and so did and said?" but also, without actually saying it, "That girl isn't really as good a friend as I am. She is not as good a person as you thought. If you have to choose, I would be the better person to have for a friend."

Gossip is one form this insecurity takes. Competition is another. Because deep down I am not sure that you will like me as I am, I hope that perhaps you will like me because of what I own or can do. We say, "Like me for my designer jeans (they are the right ones, aren't they?); like me for my new bicycle (it's faster than hers); like me for my good grades (unless it's cool not to get good grades, then I won't); like me because I'm the best athlete (my dad says I have to be the best); like me because my family goes to Hawaii in the winter; like me, like me, like me!"

People need to feel liked so that they can like themselves. Most of the ugliness in the world is inside, not outside. People know this in their spirits even when they deny it in their minds. They want desperately to feel good about themselves, to feel that they fit in, they belong, they are safe. Gossip, meanness and competition, however, ultimately only make them feel worse—

and more insecure than ever.

In recent years our society has tried to solve this problem by having people simply repeat over and over to themselves, "You are okay. You are a good person. You are beautiful as you are." But our spirits know this is a bunch of baloney. We know there is a lot of ugliness in us and that something radical must be done about it.

There is only one person whose affirmation can take that ugliness away and that is the person who made us and knows how we work. God does not affirm or ignore our ugliness, as the world would have us do. Instead he offers us forgiveness for it.

He also offers us true safety. Not an escape from the dangers and problems of living, those we have to face like anyone else, but the safety that comes from knowing and loving and being loved by the Creator of the universe. When we fully understand that God loves us, our ugliness notwithstanding, then we have the potential to like and value ourselves.

If you can start to understand this, Julie, then you will not have to gossip about your friends, nor listen to it. You will not have to compete with them. You can be glad with them for what they have and do, because your most important needs have been met by God.

Are your friends sometimes saying mean things about you when you aren't around? Perhaps. But isn't it nice not to have to worry about it?

Love, Papa

FIFTEEN

Cheating

Papa, have you
ever cheated?

Dear Nate,

YES. IN FOURTH GRADE I COPIED THE WORD PIANO off Janet Bowie's paper during a spelling test. I hadn't missed a spelling word all year and couldn't stand the thought of losing that gold star on my chart. I snapped under the pressure.

Then in eighth grade I couldn't remember what the outer ring of the sun is called. When my friend Tom Rauman whispered "corona" to someone else, I convinced myself I would have remembered it eventually anyway and wrote it down.

Is that all, you ask? Well, a few of my college term papers may have been footnoted more economically than was called for, but that was more out of ignorance than the desire to mislead anyone. And I used to be notoriously bad at calling shots in or out in tennis, but that was because I had a tendency to see the ball, well, optimistically. Besides, when I am running my eyes bounce and it's tough to make accurate calls with bouncing eyes.

Oh, do I ever cheat on anything now? Of course not. That is, not on important things. Well, perhaps I occasionally do some "creative estimating" on my taxes. That's when you're supposed to put down a figure for something which you haven't kept records on (and only a slave to organization ever would) so you have to guess. There's this powerful urge to guess in your own favor, and I may have once or twice suffered from too much creativity. But compared to most people I am a candidate for sainthood when it comes to taxes.

Hmmm. Looking over my answer, I see a disturbing pattern. The truth seems to be that I am quite willing to cheat if the situation calls for it, as long as I can convince myself that there's a reason for it, that it isn't "real cheating," and that I'm certainly no worse than and probably quite a bit better than most other people.

I stole the word *piano* because I had worked hard all year and thought I deserved my gold star. I allowed myself to use "corona" on the science test because I rationalized that I knew it anyway. I chalk my weak footnoting up to ignorance, but at times I was ignorant because I wanted to be. I keep money for myself that should go for the things we all share in this country because I convince myself that it's *mine* and that others cheat a lot more than I do.

I guess I try to distance myself from my actions. I create this space between an act that doesn't make me look good, and what I feel to be the real me. This real me insists on seeing itself as a good, even admirable person and certainly an honest one. For it to cohabit with this other person who cheats at times, it must create some wiggle room, some space from those deeds, so that it is not soiled. Do you see how this sort of splits me in two— one person to be a good fellow and the other to do the dirty work?

Nate, I am talking about integrity. Integrity means wholeness, unity. What is damaged every time I cheat is my integrity. I am no longer whole. I set one part of myself against another. I am made double—duplicitous.

And the truth is that cheating is only a superficial example of a loss of integrity. I become divided, become less, every time I choose to live my life at a lower level than God intended when he made me. And these choices, unlike spelling tests and tax returns, are offered me every day of my life.

When I was sixteen, I went to a Christian camp for boys. We had a speaker who, if I remember correctly, talked to us about sex, something of occasional interest to sixteen-year-old boys. He asked for questions at the end, and I remember working up my courage and asking if he thought it was sinful to look at "girlie" magazines—a nice distancing word.

He gave an answer which would perhaps not satisfy many moralists, but which had a great impact on me. He didn't say, as he rightfully could have, "Yes, it is a sin and God is not pleased if you do it, period!" Instead he said, "You need to decide at what plane you are going to live your life." He said more, but those are the words I remembered.

On what plane are you going to live your life? Are you going to make all the little daily compromises that most everyone else seems to make? Are you going to waver here, rationalize there, indulge yourself in this, temporarily suspend your convictions over that—until your life becomes characterized by fragmentation, halfheartedness and expedience?

The world as it is does not understand people who want to live their lives on a higher plane. They think they're either fools or saints (Mother Teresa), but either way they are out-of-touch with the so-called real world.

A trivial example: The first time I went to France, I walked out of my Paris hotel to buy a newspaper from a stand on the street. Having never used French money, I stared intently at my change as I walked away. Realizing the fellow had given me back ten francs too many, I returned immediately to the stand and tried to say he had given me too much. Thinking I was complaining about being shortchanged, the fellow adopted a surly tone (I couldn't tell what he was saying) until I simply held my hand of change out to him and he was able to see that he had given me too much. I handed him back the extra and walked away, but not before noting as great a look of incomprehension and amazement as I have seen. Nothing in the "real world," apparently, had prepared him for customers (much less Americans?) who returned excess change.

What I would suggest to you is that the real world is God's world, not the poor, perverted imitation world with which most people are satisfied. To live as fully as possible in that real world, you have to decide if you want to live on that high plane. That means being able to recognize as sin things like materialism, gossip, status-seeking and treating other people as objects (which both lust and manipulation do).

And after recognizing these and many other common actions and attitudes as sin, as things which fragment and distance you from the wholeness God intended, living in God's world means being able to say no to them. This does not mean that reading *Playboy* or lying or being unhappy until you have the latest pair of overpriced jeans or running down a friend behind her back will single-handedly destroy your life or your relationship to God. We will often do that which we hate. But I do hope that your goal, with God's help, will be to live on the highest possible plane. Life is so very short that it is a terrible waste to do anything less.

Besides, those gold stars? They're only paper.

Love, Papa

SIXTEEN

Being Somebody

This girl in my class
thinks she is so great.
She is always showing off.
Why does she do that?

Dear Matthew,

LET ME TELL YOU ABOUT MARIA. I WAS IN FOURTH OR fifth grade and went to McKinley School. It was on the southern edge of the mesa in Santa Barbara. Beyond the fence of the playground, the land fell steeply away and down below was part of a poorer section of town.

Maria lived there and every morning she walked up the long switchback paths that connected the world of her home with the world of school. And every afternoon she walked back down.

Maria was a year or two older than I was, and she was big and tough. She didn't seem afraid of anything and could even put a little fear into some of the boys. Looking back now, I think maybe she wasn't as tough as I thought.

One morning I got to school early on my bike, so I meandered out to the playground to kill time until the bell rang. I saw a big crowd of kids across the playground gathered at the gate where one of the paths came up from the neighborhood down below. The kids started to stir and make noise, and so I headed in their direction.

As I got closer I heard them shouting, "Maria! Maria!" Then they began backing up, reaching with their hands toward the middle of the crowd, yelling "Maria, give me one. Maria, over here, over here!" They were laughing and pushing each other.

As the crowd moved toward me I saw Maria in the center, her arms clutching boxes of ice cream bars and candy. She was throwing things to the kids all around her as she walked. Some were grabbing candy from her arms before she could hand it out.

I looked at her face. She smiled a little, but mostly looked serious, even a little desperate.

It was all over in less than two minutes. The crowd got smaller quickly as her store dwindled. She threw the last of it up in the air and said to the backs of the departing kids, "Sorry, it's all gone. See you again tomorrow." They didn't answer.

Even then I knew that I had just seen something very sad. I didn't know exactly why. Later, I heard she had been stealing money from her mother and stopping at a store on the way to school every morning.

It's not necessarily important that Maria was poor, though that may be why she chose ice cream and candy to get kids to like her. A lot of kids—a lot of adults—try to do the same thing in other ways. They do it because they want to be somebody, they want to count.

Your classmate who shows off and thinks she's great probably worries that maybe she isn't great at all, that maybe kids won't like her *unless* she's great. Maybe she's trying to convince herself or her parents or you.

From time to time, most of us worry about not being somebody. Maria gave away candy to make the feeling go away, but I don't think it did. Actually, there's only one thing big enough to make us feel we count over the long haul, and that's love—the love of those around us and especially the love of God for us. If God thinks we count (and he does!), then we do for sure.

So don't be too hard on your showoff classmate. She just wants to count. You can help her feel that she does.

Love, Papa

SEVENTEEN

The Power
of Reading

Papa, why do
you read so much?
Will I have to read when
I get out of school?

Dear Julie,

WHERE DO I START?

I read because of the power of words.

Through words flows the energy of the universe to create and destroy. Words have done more to shape the human experience than all the swords, guns, bombs and missiles ever made. Words are infinitely more important than money in our lives. The impoverished child who hears words of encouragement and wisdom is vastly better off than the rich child who hears only words of ridicule or neglect. God created the universe through speaking words and, in our own way, we do the same.

I read because of the insight of words.

It is largely through words, through reading, that I have discovered what I know about the world and even about myself. Those who don't know better imply that reading is an escape from reality. They say that books don't have much to do with "the real world." I have some questions for them: What is more "real," your body or your mind/spirit? Which is the greater loss, someone who has lost use of part or all of his body, or has lost use of part or all of his mind? If you are digging a ditch or selling something, are you doing something more real than if you are reading Homer? Which activity engages more of the essential you? Which has more potential for increasing your own humaneness? If books are an "escape" at all, they are an escape from the numbing superficiality of much of everyday life. They draw us toward a deeper reality.

I read because of the beauty of words.

God has made us so that when we are healthy we delight in beauty. Beauty, thankfully, is one of the truly valuable things that still cannot be bought with money. (Friendship, wisdom, love and purity are among the others.) Money can buy "ownership" of beautiful things, of course, but ownership has little to do with beauty.

Words can be beautiful in many ways. They can be beautiful in their sound, as is the sound of water in the mountains or the voice of a friend. They can be beautiful in their rhythm, like the thurumping hooves of a galloping horse. They can be beautiful in the insight they bring us, the moments of epiphany when suddenly we see what we had never seen before or feel afresh something we have always known—and in the seeing and feeling we understand more completely this world God has created and our place in it.

I read because words put me in touch with others.

Words are flares arced into the night, saying, "I am here. Is anyone else out there? Does anyone else see what I see? Feel what I feel? Hope, fear, wonder and laugh as I do?" Men and women have been sending out these flares into the darkness for thousands of years. They say to us, "This is my story. This is what happened to me and those around me. This is what I think. This is how I feel. How about you?"

For some reason I can't help being more interested in such words than I am in interest rates or promotions or raises or four-wheel drive or Michael Jackson or television preachers or Democrats and Republicans or first and goal from the two-yard line (even though I will, I admit, look up from my book to see if they pass or run) or any number of things which might be passingly interesting but are never genuinely important.

All this may be too theoretical. Let me give you one example of how one book affected my life. I don't know if it is the best example, but it comes to mind. When I was in college I read J. R. R. Tolkien's *The Lord of the Rings*. You know about Tolkien because I read you *The Hobbit* when you were very small. *The Lord of the Rings* is not one of the "great" books in human history, but it is one for which the world is a slightly better place because it was written, and that is no small thing.

The book is about mythical creatures in a mythical land doing mythical things—one of those "escape from reality" books, some would say. These creatures, though largely invented by the power of Tolkien's imagination, correspond closely with the kind of people we find within and around us. Although there are wizards and heroes here and there in the book, most are sort of common, garden-variety creatures like ourselves.

The garden-variety creatures, however, find themselves in a world contested over by the forces of good and evil. They find they cannot hide in their comfortable hobbit holes but are forced to make choices, take action, risk dangers, often in situations where the right choice, action or risk is not at all clear.

I read this at a time in my life when I, like many my age, was trying to figure out my own place in the world. These mythical little creatures in this good but not great book made me admire something I saw very little of in the "real world." They caused me to value moral courage. Through the power and insight and beauty of Tolkien's words, they made me want more than anything to be on the side of good in life. They also made me realize how difficult that could be, how good and evil are often mixed together in individuals and situations and yet how, nonetheless, choices must be made and genuine action taken.

Simply put, I proposed to be a better person because of a single book, and I don't think that proposition has been totally without fruit.

I cannot talk about books, however, without pointing out that as followers of God, we are "people of the book." That is an old phrase that points out the centrality of the written word, God's revelation in the Bible, to those who claim him. It is of the greatest importance that God chose *words* as the primary way to communicate to his creation. Even the Incarnation, God showing himself to us and sharing our experience in Jesus Christ, is preserved in words for those of us who were not there.

Should we only read the Bible, then, as a few suggest? No. God gave the power and insight and beauty of words to all healthy men and women, both to those who acknowledge him and those who don't. (It may be one of the many ways in which we are made in the image of God.) Words, like all things, can be perverted and used for evil, but when they speak truth and beauty they should be prized, whatever their source. For all truth and beauty come ultimately from God.

"Will I have to read books when I am out of school?" you ask. The better question is, "Will I be fortunate enough to read books once I am out of school?" You do not have to read the books I read, but if you read hardly at all, or if you read only to kill time rather than enrich it, you will impoverish your life in a way that no amount of money can amend.

In fact, why not put down this letter and look around for a good book, one with power and insight and beauty.

Love, Papa

EIGHTEEN

Families: Required Membership

Papa, everybody
in this family is bugging me.
Can I get out?

Dear Matthew,

I'M SORRY, BUT TRYING TO GET OUT OF A FAMILY IS sort of like Jonah trying to get out of going to where God sent him. You can head the opposite way, but somehow all directions lead back to Nineveh.

Your family is part of the cards you are dealt in life, just like the freckles on your nose and the brown of your eyes. Your family is there. You didn't ask for them; they didn't ask, specifically, for you. For better and for worse, you are a part of each other.

I think it's mostly for better. The difference between you being in our family and a hand of cards is that your presence is not by chance. God has put you among us for your benefit and for ours. This is true even when Nate is eating your popcorn while you're out going to the bathroom (despite your telling him you had counted all the kernels and would break his neck if any were missing).

Being in a family should help you discover all of the following:

who you are, who you want to be, who you can be and who you ought to be. Sometimes there are powerful conflicts between these different things, but a family should be a place where powerful conflicts can safely take place.

Families are difficult places to be in, often, because it is in our families that we most fully indulge our human weaknesses. If we were our obnoxiously undiluted selves in public the way we are with family, life would be a series of broken noses. One definition of "home" is the place where you can be a complete jerk and they will still call you for dinner.

You shouldn't expect the people in your family to always understand you. Why should they? You often don't understand yourself. The people in your family are both like you and not like you. You are much more like us, Matthew, than you realize. That will not become clear to you until years from now when you have been away and other people point out the similarities.

But we are also not like each other. You are a unique creation, Matthew, as are Julie, Nate and your mom and I. When God made each of us, he imagined someone new, someone whom even *he* hadn't quite thought of before. That is wonderful, but it can cause problems. Combine your uniqueness with your fallenness (we are sinners all) and you have the ingredients for that familiar cry of young and old alike: "No one understands me!"

And no one, short of God, does fully understand you. But families should be places where "not understanding" leads to patience, acceptance and discussion, not to rejection. In some cases, a family may never understand, but it should always be glad to see you walking through the door (as I am glad to see each of my children) at the end of the day.

If our families sometimes don't understand us, more often they understand us too well. Our families bug us because they know all our tricks. They know what our next line is going to be, maybe because we got the line from them. We can't fake them out like we do outsiders. How can you pretend to be a model of selflessness if everyone in the family remembers the year you ate *all* the leftover apple pie the morning after Thanksgiving?

It is a basic human desire to be known and valued, but it's irritating to be known too well. That's why evil loves the darkness. The nice thing about families, when they are working right, is that they can know you all too well and still think it's pretty great having you be a part of them. Your family can say to you, "Those aren't freckles. They're beauty marks—and you got them from your great-grandfather Sam."

Which brings up an important fact. You aren't just part of one family in your life, but at least three or four and in a sense many others. You are part of the family you are born into, but that family is already a part of two others, that of your mother's and of mine. What we are as a family is intimately and inescapably tied in with what those other families are and have been. Likewise you will probably one day make a family of your own, joining in the process with the family of whomever you marry. You are likely then to have children who will one day have their own families, drawing you along into yet more family relationships.

Family is one of the fundamental givens of human experience. It is to our advantage to do all that we can to make it a positive force in our lives. I encourage you, even while you are young, to value your family. That brother and sister who are now rivals for the extra dessert are also people who have shared a part of your life that no one you ever meet will have shared. They will have contributed to making you what you are, just as you are influencing who they are becoming.

Speak encouragement to them then, as often as you can. Tell

them how well they are doing and how much fun they are to be around. Leave a little apple pie for them, and they will leave some popcorn for you. And then, someday, you will look forward eagerly to the times you can be together. You will recall the time we saw *Romeo and Juliet* played on motorcycles and with dark glasses in London. You will laugh about "Uncle" Owen's handkerchief rabbit, and you will cry, perhaps, over things that are yet to come in our lives together.

But most of all, you will be thankful that there are people to whom you belong, who love you even when they can't stand what you're doing, who can't think of what they are or what life is without thinking of you. That's a great thing, and it's present even in many families that are all messed up in a lot of ways.

Sisters, brothers, mothers and fathers can all be a pain in the neck. But they are also one of God's best ideas. When he thought of families he thought of us—and I, for one, am very glad.

Love, Papa

NINETEEN

Serious Laughter

Papa, why do you
and Mom laugh so much?

Dear Nate,

IT COULD BE THAT WE LAUGH SO MUCH BECAUSE YOUR mother and I are both incredibly witty. Or it might be just that we have low standards.

I haven't given much thought to why we laugh. Laughter tends to disappear if you analyze it too much. Perhaps frequent laughter is one way in which we affirm life. It is a way of saying that it is good to be alive, even if life is painful. It says life is still interesting, there are still surprises, there are things in which we can delight.

All people laugh, of course, but I think the Christian view of the world is especially well suited to laughter. For the Christian, life is ultimately a comedy, not a tragedy. I am using *comedy* in its highest and oldest sense, as a story with a happy ending. Christians believe in a happy ending. Despite the presence of great suffering and evil in the world, we believe that God is bending the arc of human history toward redemption. He is in the process of redeeming his creation. Evil and death were defeated at Calvary and—miracle of miracles—all shall be well. This is a view of life that promotes healthy laughter.

Laughter is, I think, literally a gift of God. It may even be part of what it means to be made in God's image. We can laugh because God does.

Laughter contains within it many elements important to the Christian life together: joy, community, surprise, creativity, confession. Healthy laughter is a shared experience of a moment of joy. It does not have to spring from something momentous; an unexpected bit of verbal creativity is enough. It can also reflect a needed recognition of our own shortcomings, foolishness and failure.

Laughter, in this latter sense, can be a great instrument of realism. It reminds us that we are always and only human beings, subject to illusions and delusions of every kind. It helps us fit our hats.

It is a common mistake to think that comedy and laughter are not serious. This is not true at all. Not only is comedy at the heart of the Christian vision of reality, but laughter and suffering are often closely linked. A fair part of my last days with my friend Jon before his death were spent laughing. Phyllis did not think the pain of cancer precluded the joy of shared laughter at the comedy of life and the hope of Christian death. And the laughter was not exactly *despite* the pain; it was somehow linked to it.

There is, of course, a perverted version of all good things. Healthy laughter accepts, celebrates, heals and unifies. Perverted laughter rejects, wounds, condemns and divides. I know this because I have been the instrument of wounding laughter in people's lives. It began in the weakness and insecurity of adolescence and lasted longer than it should have. I have not totally overcome it.

I am glad that in our home one hears frequent laughter. It is a blessing. I encourage you to laugh a lot in life. There is much to celebrate and to delight in. But do not be mockers, for in mockery there is no celebration or delight. Make your laughter an affirmation of creation and of others.

Love, Papa

TWENTY

Boyfriends and Girlfriends

Papa, did you ever have
girlfriends when you were a kid?
Do you think it's good
to have a girlfriend or boyfriend
when you're growing up?

Dear children,

*YES, I HAD LOTS OF GIRLFRIENDS WHEN I WAS GROW-*ing up. I just never let any of them know about it.

Seems like every year as I moved from school to school there was someone who I felt especially shy around and that was the feeling I associated with love.

In first grade in Lubbock it was a little girl with beautiful, long blond hair and braces on her legs. She'd had polio and wore heavy leather and metal braces that I found intriguing. Maybe I liked her because I felt sorry for her, but I think it was more because she was quiet and gentle and pretty.

In fourth and fifth grades, when we lived in Santa Barbara, I secretly yearned for Janet because Janet could hit a ball as hard as any of the boys and next to me was the fastest kid in the class. I don't know whether I would have liked her as much if she had been faster than me. Boys are funny that way.

Janet had blond hair too. She wore it in a pony tail and when she ran it streamed behind her like the tail of a horse. I thought that was grand.

I never admitted to liking her or any other girl. But sometimes I would ride down her street, even though it was out of my way, in hopes of seeing her in the yard. If I did see her, I was likely to ride by looking the other way. It was a kind of courtship ritual, I guess.

We used to square dance in school. I never would choose Janet for a square-dancing partner because then everyone would know. But I remember angling to get into her square so that I could be close. When we went around the circle taking in turn the hand of each of the girls, I would look ahead and see her coming and feel a kind of lump in my throat. Sometimes I allowed myself a small smile as I took her hand, but she was often looking away herself.

The first time I could be accused of liking a girl without denying it was in eighth grade, though even then I wouldn't admit to having an official "girlfriend." Her name was Tina. Believe it or not, that name had a powerful ring to it then.

That was the year we lived in Lakewood, California. Those kids were a little faster than I was used to. They listened to rock music while all I listened to were Dodger games. They had parties without an adult in sight; my idea of a wild time had been filching extra pie at church potluck dinners.

Everyone worked real hard at matching me up with Tina. The only thing that was clear to me was that she, being a lot closer to being a woman than I was to being a man, was more than I could handle.

I made it a policy never to go over to her house without a friend along. One day, when I wasn't paying attention, my escort left and I found myself alone with Tina. I suddenly realized how wise I had been all those years to have never admitted to liking a girl. Here I was alone with one. I called to mind the story of

Joseph and Potiphar's wife. Fortunately, she was too busy laughing at me to be a threat to my virtue.

We moved again soon after that. The scare with Tina was enough to keep me away from girls until I got to college. Throughout high school I traveled with small packs of quasi-adolescent males, mostly bouncing, passing, kicking and hitting balls of one shape or another. It was a good way to get through a very dangerous period of life.

Do I think it's okay to have a girlfriend or boyfriend when growing up? Sure. I hope you aren't as uneasy with the opposite sex as I was. From what I can see, it doesn't seem you are.

It is great to feel that one person is special for a while and to be brave and confident enough to admit it. A boy can learn a lot from a girl—especially how not to be such a selfish jerk. I don't know what girls can learn from guys, except maybe to stick up for themselves when someone else *is* being a selfish jerk.

I wouldn't let romance be too big a part of all this. Romance is for later (when you are fifty or so, I think). Boyfriends and girlfriends when you are young are there to enjoy, to feel special about, to tell things to, to laugh with and, inevitably, to break up with. Breaking up is an important part. It lets you feel some emotions that boys especially don't feel often enough, and it lets you find that there are other people to feel special about.

All this is good. It's part of the pleasure of life. Do learn from my mistake—if you like someone, ask them to square dance!

Love, Papa

TWENTY-ONE

Ummm... Sex

What about,
uh, sex,
Papa?

Dear children,

I'M BUSY RIGHT NOW. ASK YOUR MOTHER.

Love, Papa

No, Papa, really. We know all about how it's done. You don't have to tell us that. But, well, a lot of kids our age are experimenting with it right now. What do you think?

D ear children-who-are-growing-up-too-fast,

YOU'RE RIGHT. WE NEED TO TALK ABOUT THIS.
Please forgive my being uncomfortable here. You have to realize
something about my generation. Our parents were raised not to
talk about these things. So my parents didn't talk to me. But
somewhere in the middle of my adolescence, suddenly everyone
was *required* to talk about these things—and not only talk. You
didn't want to look like you were afraid of the subject, so people
became afraid to appear afraid. Therefore, they began to babble
about it endlessly.

It doesn't seem to me that all the talking and doing has
improved things much. But that's not what you asked about.

Let's see. Perhaps I'll just begin by saying straight out that I
think sex was made for marriage—not for before, beside or in-
between. You probably already know that this is a very old-
fashioned view. It's a pretty easy view to make fun of, in fact. If

you decide to make it your view, you should expect some people to think you are stupid—but I can think of worse things.

My view of sex, as of most things, is shaped by my belief that God made the world and every good thing in it. God made our sexuality part of his creation for many reasons. From a practical point of view, it's the way to make sure there are always more kids like you guys. God could have created a human photocopy machine that makes all-color, double-sided copies of each of us. Or he could have made us so we just sort of split in two and reproduce ourselves that way.

But neither of those would be as much fun as sex. And, believe it or not, God likes fun. In fact, he invented it. Just look at some of the animals he made and you know he has a sense of humor. Look at us, for that matter.

Sex is supposed to be fun, then, as well as practical. But fun isn't really a strong enough word. Skiing is fun. Monopoly is fun. Writing these letters to you is fun. But sex, as God designed it, is something more than that.

It's almost like making love with the person you marry is symbolic of our relationship with God. I don't want to push that too far. Believe me, even most people who love God are not thinking a lot about him at the moment they are making love. But that's okay because God wants them thinking about each other then. He wants them thinking about how much they love each other, even if they've been fighting that day or if they are getting on each other's nerves (in fact, especially then).

He wants them telling each other with their bodies as well as in other ways that it's all right, that they still are loved even if neither of them deserves it. He wants them thinking about how they can give each other pleasure, how they can show that they care that the other is alive and belongs to them.

And that's not too far off from what God wants in *his*

relationship to us. Maybe one of the reasons God gave us sex then is to give us a way of understanding what passionate commitment and tenderness and selflessness and sharing could be like. Unfortunately we often turn sex into the opposite of these things—lust, aggression, selfishness and so on. And that's just another reason why we need grace and forgiveness and healing.

Maybe you're wondering, "If sex is fun and can help us understand and practice good things, then why should people only do this in marriage? Why shouldn't they practice these things with lots of people? You know what they say, 'Practice makes perfect.' "

Very clever, kids, very clever. Actually it's a pretty good question. It even makes "sense," especially if one is looking for a justification to do what one is already determined to do anyway. And my answer won't satisfy a lot of up-to-date people. But I think it's true.

The old reason given for waiting until marriage was that God said so. That's a pretty good reason. But these days people are quite impressed with their own minds, and a lot of them don't care what anybody else says, not even the one who made them. "God says so" isn't good enough for them.

I think it's perfectly all right, then, to ask ourselves, "Why might the one who made us have known that it was best that we not have sex with just anyone who our hormones identified as a likely target?" Or, to put it more charitably, why not even with two or three others during the course of a lifetime?

These days you could make a good case just by talking about sexual diseases, unwanted babies, broken families and many other consequences of sleeping around. But I think there's more to it than that. I think it has something to do with God knowing us better than we know ourselves.

God made us. He knows how our mind and heart and spirit work. He knows what will ultimately (not just in the next thirty minutes) make us happy, whole and secure. He knows that we need to be loved, not just liked; that we need to give love, not just receive it; that these needs are basic to what it means to be human and to be made in the image of God. And he knows how profoundly these things are connected to our sexuality.

He also knows how disastrous it is when these things are abused. Sex is not the only way these needs are met, but it is one of the most powerful, even dangerous ways, and marriage is the context God has provided for that power to be released. It's the only thing potentially strong enough to contain the forces that sex sets in motion. Marriage doesn't guarantee that sex will be all it should be; it is simply the place where it *can* work as its creator intended.

Something happens when we try to use sex apart from marriage. We both reduce it and distort it. It becomes a thing of mere curiosity or self-gratification or obsession or a way of hiding insecurities or of controlling someone else. It can still be "fun"—for a while—but it comes at a very high price. More often than not, that fun is simply a down payment on a lot of pain.

But I don't want to just say, "Wait on sex, otherwise you'll get in a lot of trouble." I want to say, "Wait on sex, because God has made us so that waiting and committing are consistent with what is best for us, with our greatest happiness, with the best of what it means to be human beings created in his image."

God wants us to have the most profound spiritual and physical union with one other person. Such a thing can happen only over a lifetime. If one partner dies, it can sometimes happen a second time. It can't, however, happen every weekend with a different person. It can't even happen with the person you have "dated" for six months or a year, even if you "plan to get married." It certainly can't happen with one person while you are married to another.

By intending us only to have one partner, maybe God wanted to illustrate something about our relationship with him. The Bible tells us God is a jealous God. He's not jealous in the way we are sometimes. It means, however, that God expects us to be committed to him. He doesn't want us "sleeping around" with other gods or committed to other things that become the reason for which we live.

The Bible tells us that we are in a sense married to Christ. One measure of our ability to be faithful to Christ is our ability to be faithful, sexually and otherwise, to the person he has given us in marriage.

I know that bringing our relationship to God into all this may seem a little irrelevant to what you are facing. We are dealing with hormones and the shapes of bodies and the back seats of cars. But I guess I want you to do some thinking *before* you get in the back seat. Make some decisions while you are thinking clearly that you can call to mind when your thought processes are more muddled. Decide what you think about yourself and your body and your Maker and that person you will someday marry. Decide why *you* think God made sex and why he has told us to wait.

You can still have a lot of fun with someone special—without compromising what God has made both of you for.

Love, Papa

TWENTY-TWO

Proving God

Papa, I hope it's okay for us to ask
this question. It makes us nervous
even to think about it.

How do we know for certain there
really is a God? A lot of people
don't think there is.

How can we prove we are right?

Dear children,

THE SHORT ANSWER IS "WE DON'T" AND "WE CAN'T."
But, I want to quickly add, that's because that is the way God wants it.

You have to ask yourself what you mean by words like *for certain* and *prove*. If *for certain* means "absolutely no possibility of being wrong," and *prove* means "evidence that no human being can possibly reject," then no, we cannot be certain or prove that God exists and is who the Bible tells us he is.

Is this a bad thing? I don't think so. *We* may wish it were otherwise, but I don't think God does.

If God wants us to believe in him and do as he says, why doesn't he just appear to us and show himself to be God so that there is absolutely no mistaking that he's in charge? (Maybe he could play for the Chicago Cubs and hit 1.000 and lead them to a World Series Championship—now that would be proof!)

One answer people have given to this question (which usually leaves out the Cubs) is that God wants to be loved and worshiped freely. God has created us as creatures with free wills. That means we can make choices. We choose to do this and not that. Someone else chooses to do that and not this. Both have to accept the consequences of the choices they make.

This freedom is both wonderful and terrible. It is wonderful because it accounts for the rich complexity and creativity of human life. If we didn't have choices we would essentially be robots—efficient but ultimately boring. It is terrible because we are free to choose wrongly, even disastrously. We can choose evil in all its many subtle forms, from hatred to indifference and, most foolish of all, we can choose to ignore the God who made us.

Because God wants us to respond to him freely, he does not overpower us with his presence. He does not appear to us in our bedrooms, eight feet tall with a fierce look and a deep, booming voice, saying, "I am!" (at least not in my bedroom so far). If he did, I would certainly do whatever he said, but I'm not sure that it would bring God the kind of honor that he deserves. God prefers that we seek and serve him because of our recognition that he is the source of all that is good and true and beautiful and because he has given each of us the opportunity to know him.

That's one answer for why God doesn't show himself unmistakably to men and women. But I doubt it is all the answer. Another part of it is that God, in his wisdom and goodness, does what he wants to do, and he doesn't always tell us why. God is not us and we can only barely begin to understand what he is. This is not a cop-out so we won't have to wrestle with difficult questions; it is simply a fact. One result of this fact is that we cannot "explain" everything. I like it that way (a totally "explained" life is a very dull one), but others find this very bothersome.

Some people who do not believe in God take this unexplainability as proof that God doesn't exist. That isn't good logic, but it keeps them from having to answer some difficult questions of their own. Some Christians respond by insisting that they *can* in fact explain *everything*. Without realizing it, they are really more or less agreeing with the skeptics that lack of total proof is devastating to belief.

I think both of them are wrong. The most important things in life, while they sometimes involve reason, almost never involve proof or certainty. All things of great value require us to take chances, to risk being wrong: love between two people, creating a work of art, building a friendship, working for justice in the world, trying to help someone in trouble. Even businesspeople know this.

Why should we expect it to be different with God? He has created us, and he wants us to know him. He has communicated with us in one way or another since the beginning of time. He has revealed himself to us in the Bible. And, most amazingly of all, he has come to be one of us and suffer with us in the person of Jesus Christ.

But he hasn't taken away our freedom to reject him. He has the power to compel everyone to acknowledge and obey him. He has chosen not to use that power. That choice is rooted in the very essence of who God is. One of the greatest evidences of true power is the choice not to use it. This is something human beings rarely understand.

Having argued that certainty and proof are not particularly relevant to faith in God, or most important things in life, I want to say very clearly that there is a tremendous amount of evidence that the God of the Bible is who he says. The evidences are of all kinds: philosophical, historical, psychological, experiential and more.

But we human beings are not nearly as logical and reasonable as we often pretend. All of us, including Christians, are capable of ignoring anything that is inconvenient for what we want to do or believe. The Bible tells us a man could come back from the dead to warn his brothers about hell and they wouldn't believe him (hell being a very inconvenient idea).

God allows us the freedom to be wrong, to not believe, to live life as though there are only these few years and nothing else. The only "proof" that will finally overcome this is the proof of a convicted heart (I include the mind in that), and that conviction only comes through the diverse work of the Holy Spirit in the lives of individual men and women, boys and girls.

If you sometimes wonder if God is there at all, don't worry. God is not bothered by that, even though your fellow believers sometimes will be. He understands struggle and pain because in Christ he felt them both.

It reminds me a little of what your cousin Jonathan asked his parents when he was about six. "Do you think," he asked, "that Santa Claus knows that we know he isn't real?" When we sometimes doubt the existence or goodness of God, we often do so with a similar kind of superficial disbelief. The huge difference is that God is not Santa Claus. He is the creator of the universe, the source of all that is good and true and beautiful and, wonder of wonders, he knows and loves each of you. Whether our doubts are superficial or very deep he waits patiently, showing us his love even while we are unlovely.

Some of the greatest servants of God have doubted him. But they have also persevered. And they have continued to take risks for their faith, even as they questioned. I would encourage this for you as well: have faith, ask questions, take risks.

Love, Papa

TWENTY-THREE

Poor
People

Papa, what about poor people?
Shouldn't we do something
to help them?

Dear Julie,

AH, YES—THE POOR. WELL OF COURSE WE SHOULD HELP them all we can—and we do. That is to say, we try to. Well, perhaps not *"all* we can," but certainly a lot more than most. . . . I mean we do give money . . . and there was the time. . . .

Hmmm. It's sort of complicated. Let me tell you a story. Not long ago your mom and I went to a play in London. It is called *Les Miserables* and is a musical based on a famous novel by a Frenchman named Victor Hugo. Many, many people wanted to see this musical. It was sold out for weeks ahead, and long lines waited to buy any tickets that might be returned.

We had been fortunate earlier in the day to buy two tickets at an agency that told us these tickets had been reserved for some of their elite customers but had been returned. They only cost forty-five dollars a piece. It was our lucky day.

When we arrived at our seats that night we found that we were, indeed, among the elite. The clothes sitting around us were very fine, the diamonds large and bright, the expressions on faces self-consciously sophisticated. I was particularly intrigued by a woman who sat in front of us. She was in her forties, elegantly dressed and bejeweled, with a matching husband. She was in her element but not at ease. When the lights went down for the beginning of the play she put on stylish but exceedingly thick glasses.

Les Miserables is a story about the poor and society's attitudes toward them. Many of the poor in it are very virtuous, an idea which those who are not poor are very willing to concede. This musical adaptation of the novel was put on by the Royal Shakespeare Company, and they know how to put on a good show. There were grand sets, a revolving stage, touching songs and heroic deaths. During the rousing final number, when even the heroic dead were on their feet singing, I noticed the woman in front wiping her eyes and blowing her nose. A good time was had by all.

In a sense, the show continued outside. Your mom and I stood around on the London sidewalk watching the playgoers stream to their limousines and taxis. There was something intriguing about the scattering of the well-to-do on the crowded streets of the London theater district on a Friday night.

But while we watched, we saw something that broke the spell. Right in front of the theater, surrounded on every side by fashionable people hurrying into the night, was a bum going through a trash can. He was fairly young, I would say in his thirties, but in every other way fit the stereotype of the back-alley bum: dirty, shabbily dressed, seemingly in some kind of stupor.

As soon as I noticed the bum I also saw that he was being yelled at by a driver of one of the taxis waiting for a theater patron. The driver (not a native Englishman, for what it's worth) was out of his cab, shouting at this fellow that he was a disgrace and should be ashamed. He told him to get out so these people didn't have to see him and then gave him a kick. A few seconds later the woman with the big diamonds and thick glasses came by on her way to her limousine, her husband safely in tow. She didn't seem to notice anything, maybe because her glasses were once again hidden away.

A lot of questions went through my mind and still do. If the rich woman had noticed the driver kicking the bum, would she have seen any connection between the play that had just moved her to tears and the scene in front of her on the street? Why was the taxi driver offended by this fellow going through the trash? Was he *more* offended because it was happening in front of his potential customers? Did he think it was going to hurt his business or was he simply disgusted by people who didn't work for a living like he did?

And what about me? Why did I say nothing when this guy gave the bum a kick? Was I momentarily paralyzed by surprise? Was I afraid if I said anything the guy might kick me? Would I have done something, as I told myself I would, if he had kicked him a second time (or would I have waited for a third)?

This little scene contains, I think, many of the elements of the problem of poverty in our society. First, poverty is the exception, not the norm. (It's the other way around in many other parts of the world.) Most people are not poor, and they have a lot happening in their lives. They have taxis to get to.

Second, we would prefer the poor to stay out of sight. Most people wouldn't protest this bum going through the trash, but it was kind of tacky of him to do it right in front of all these people who had just had a good time seeing a musical about the virtuous poor. Little about this guy made you want to hum the theme song.

And also, there are some people who, for whatever reasons—prejudice, the need for power, financial gain—actively oppress the poor. These are relatively few in number.

Then there is the audience. There is both the woman who, with her glasses off, doesn't want to know and there is me, who observes and reflects and has all the right opinions about what he is observing—and does nothing.

And what would have been the right thing to do? Give the taxi driver a kick so that he could see how it feels? Give the bum a hundred dollars? Take him to a nearby restaurant and buy him some food? Tell him about Jesus and hope the words would penetrate the fog in his brain?

I don't know even now what the best response would have been (though I'm quite sure mine was not it), but a few things have occurred to me. One is that the bum was not the only impoverished person in that scene. He was materially and perhaps mentally poor. The man who kicked him and those who were the audience suffered, however, from another kind of poverty. The rich woman suffered from her seeming inability to transfer her stage-emotion to the real world; the driver from prizing the favor of the rich above the humanity of the poor; and I, perhaps worst of all, from preferring detached observation to risky involvement.

Therefore be careful of thinking too narrowly about poverty. Beware of thinking you are in a position to do the poor great favors. Do not assume that they necessarily need more of what you have to give them than you need what some of them can give you.

The richest man in Minnesota was quoted as saying that the single best way of judging a man was by determining the amount of money he had. This is a very common but extremely foolish idea. Think of money as sea shells, as it is in some cultures, and you will begin to see how stupid this is. Would we necessarily envy or admire the man who had huge piles of sea shells in his back yard? Would we eagerly trade the brief years of our lives in order to have a bigger pile of shells than our neighbor?

We all are poor in some way or other. The person who thinks money is the measure of success suffers from a kind of poverty of the imagination and intellect as well as of the spirit. Others suffer a kind of poverty of the emotions, unable to intertwine their lives affirmingly with the lives of others. And the Bible tells us we are all poor before God. God offers us all of creation and a relationship with him and we have only our brokenness to offer back. (Thankfully, that is all that he requires.)

All this is not an attempt to dismiss our responsibility to the materially poor or to justify my passive observation that night at the theater. It is, rather, an appeal to consider carefully who the poor are and what the Christian response to poverty is.

The Bible makes clear that by far the most serious kind of poverty is spiritual poverty and that this poverty afflicts people of every race, class, nationality, age and sex. It offers as the solution for this poverty a right relationship with God through Jesus Christ.

But the Bible also has much to say about material poverty, and it is clearly on the side of the poor. Poverty in the Bible is rarely attributed, as we usually like to do, to laziness or wickedness on the part of the poor. Much more often it is seen as the product of injustice or greed or mercilessness on the part of those who have much. The Bible repeatedly promises heavy consequences for those who insist on increasing the pile of their own sea shells while ignoring the needs of the poor.

Is money the root of all evil? No. The love of money is. But we shouldn't rest too easily because of that distinction. We show what we love by that to which we most happily devote our attention. The television shows we watch, the fantasies we rehearse in our minds and the earnestness with which we seek to increase our pile of shells all testify to where our hearts too often are.

Money is a morally neutral human invention with great potential for evil and a lesser but genuine potential for good (it is lesser because the truly valuable things in life have so little to do with it). How much comes your way over the years is not very important. What attitude you take toward it is.

Part of that attitude should be that money has come your way in order to meet genuine, God-created needs—your own and others. Whether you receive much or little of this human commodity, you should not close your hand around it tightly. Receive as much as life sends your way, but pass most of it on to others and never consider it a measure of who you are.

And we do have a biblical responsibility to pass some of that on to the so-called poor. That is not to be taken lightly or rationalized away. But I think we have a much greater responsibility to the poor than even this: to allow the poor the dignity of their individual lives as children of God. We must see them first as individual human beings, not members of a class, not "projects" through which we can alleviate our guilt, not weak unfortunates who need help from us—the "strong."

The poor are much more like us than not. Some are weak, some are strong; some are lazy and evil; most work far harder than the affluent ever will; some are likeable, others are clods. Most are people who, like me, are trying to find meaning and peace and love in a world that seems short of these things. And are they less successful in this pursuit than the rest of us? Do the poor know less about love and family and laughter and friendship and faith?

I would be slow to say so. Do the poor have anything, ever, to give to us? Is it always clear who the poor are and who are the rich?

Yes, Julie, we should help the poor. Yes, the poor must help us as well. In writing this letter, it has occurred to me what perhaps I should have done when I saw that bum outside the theater. I should have asked him his name.

Love, Papa

TWENTY-FOUR

The Woman
to Marry

Papa, what kind of woman
should we marry?

Dear Matthew and Nate,

THE EASY (AND TRUTHFUL) ANSWER IS SOMEONE LIKE your mother. But since she's too tired to go through another marriage, you will have to find someone who *approximates* her qualities.

Marry a woman with a certain vitality for living. As a Taylor male, you have inherited an unusual number of sloth genes. This is not so apparent now while you are young. They generally start kicking in around the age of twenty-eight and then it's basically a question thereafter of whether you will die in your bed taking a nap or on the couch watching television. As irritating as energetic people often can be, you will *need* someone with an enthusiasm for living. (Someone has to prod you into changing positions on the couch so that you don't get bedsores.) Avoid a woman whose idea of camping is a beautiful view of the mountain from a hotel suite. It's also a bad sign if she has great aversion to getting her hair wet.

Marry a woman with curiosity. If she doesn't wonder about

a lot of things, you should wonder about her. She should be a person who is willing to take risks, both for herself and for and with you, in order to accomplish significant ends. (Not the least of which is simply to keep life interesting.) She doesn't actually have to be willing to start a goat farm in Algeria with you (lie back down on the couch and that impulse will go away), but somewhere deep inside her the idea should be at least mildly intriguing.

Marry a woman who you could picture never getting married and still having a full life. Marriage is a good and natural thing, and right for most people. But a woman who would feel fragmented or that her life would be a failure unless she finds someone to marry her is not promising. She lacks the sense of self necessary to make a good marriage partner.

Marry a woman who gives affectionate encouragement easily. You and your children are both going to need it. (Do not forget that she and they will need it from you as well.) Do not be afraid to expect that your wife be capable of unbegrudging nurturing. It is not fashionable these days to expect that of women. I think you should still seek it in a wife. The new part is that you should expect it in yourself as well. If neither of you has it, don't have children.

Marry a woman who has genuine spiritual sensitivity, not just the right beliefs about God. It is unfortunate that in our time women have become the primary keepers of the spiritual flame. (This is true even though religious leaders are still mostly men.) Unfortunate because of what is lost when half of the leadership in a family hasn't much of a clue as to where to lead. In our marriage, your mother kept alive a pursuit of the things of God during times when I was pursuing secondary matters.

She still is the one who talks to you children most often and naturally about God and spiritual things. She weaves them into the daily details of our lives together because they are woven into her own. I have learned more than I can articulate from her about the determined pursuit of God, but I have not learned to manifest this easily or reflexively in everyday exchanges. This is a great failing on my part, but one whose negative influence on you has been lessened, I hope, by God having had the grace to provide me with a spiritually sensitive partner.

Marry a woman with right priorities. She can like, even desire, "nice things," but she should understand clearly where those things stand in order of importance. They cannot in any way be a key to her contentment. If they are, contentment will always elude her and therefore you.

She should have the potential for integrity, for wholeness. She may not have it initially because the young are often fragmented. But you should have confidence that it is toward wholeness and maturity that she is headed. It is helpful if she is a little bit ahead of you in this regard, for American men are notoriously slow in maturing. She can hold things together for a while if it takes you longer to get over being a little boy.

Finally, marry a woman who can laugh. She'll need it. And so will you.

I did not set out to describe your mother, but I have. God's unmerited favor toward me is nowhere more clear than in allowing me Jayne for my wife. Like I said at the beginning, you should marry your mother. Since that's not possible, the next best thing is to bring potential candidates by the house. Your mom is likely to make known, subtly of course, which is the right one.

God bless.

Love, Papa

TWENTY-FIVE

The Man
to Marry

Papa, what kind of man
should I marry?

Dear Julie,

YOU WILL HAVE WON HALF THE BATTLE IF YOU actually wait to marry a *man*—instead of one of the many boys (of all ages) who are walking down the aisles these days. Of course, based on that criterion, your mother would have been single for a lot longer than she was.

I write this letter with more than a little skepticism. Would a young woman, let alone an adolescent girl, actually listen to her father on matters of the heart? Can rational argument and sage advice compete with dreamy blue eyes and powerful emotions? I don't know, but at least I'll have my say. I'm going to make this as practical as I can.

Marry a man who will talk to you.

This may seem a strange and unnecessary piece of advice, but it isn't. Women want nothing more, in my experience, than to have their isolation pierced. All human beings, by the very fact of our individuality, exist naturally in a kind of isolation or aloneness. Men, for whatever reasons, have tended to adapt to that isolation, to almost take it for granted. Women, being superior creatures in many ways, usually resist it. They send out messages: "I am here. . . . I need someone else. . . . Is anyone there?"

I know what I'm talking about here because I am one of those men who is too comfortable with isolation. I can remember that when I lived alone in graduate school I went days at a time without speaking more than a few words—and not thinking it strange or undesirable. Earlier, I recall being shocked when a young woman I dated in college told me I was boring (or something like that) because I rarely revealed what, if anything, was going on in my head. (Boring, *moi*?)

It won't be enough to find a fellow who is intelligent. Intelligence and the desire to commune are two very different things. And don't necessarily take your dating life as the only gauge. Many is the man who bares his soul in prom night exchanges who becomes a preoccupied, torporous couch potato after a few months of marriage.

Clues to keep an eye out for include: How does his father relate to his mother? How does he relate to his mother? What is his general attitude toward women? What degree of respect does he show for your own intelligence and insight? Is he curious *about you*? Find a man who cares enough to penetrate to where you really *live*.

Second, Julie, marry a man who has at least a few clues as to what life is all about. He doesn't have to have all the answers (in fact, watch out for that kind!), but he should have a healthy curiosity and a few strong hunches.

If a man is not curious about life, he is going to be boring to live with. That curiosity has to extend beyond the fascination of making and spending money. He should neither under nor overestimate the importance of making a living in the world. He should realize that a living has to be made, but should also know that making money does not make a life. (Having said this, he should definitely plan on making enough to support his father-in-law in old age, should that become necessary.)

Look for somebody capable of being excited by an idea. If he is primarily interested in *things,* then he is more likely to see those around him as mere things.

And of course, the central "idea" in life is the reality of God. If you marry a man who does not understand this, then you are insuring a life of recurring pain at the deepest levels. Follow the biblical injunction here about being yoked equally together, and you will never regret it. It will be difficult enough to pull through your life together when you are pulling in approximately the same direction; much more difficult if your most fundamental understanding about the nature of reality is drastically different.

And mere acknowledgement of the reality of God is not enough. Marry, if you can find one, a man who has some genuine sensitivity about and hunger for spiritual things. Our churches are filled with men who believe the right things but whose daily lives show no inclination for the things of God. They have neither spiritual curiosity nor courage.

Having said this, let me warn you however about the spiritual overlords—men with all the answers about the things of God and the assurance that *they,* finally, will run a family the way God has always intended. Their desire to be in charge has nothing to do with the biblical injunction to lead, and it will require a fair bit of discernment on your part to tell the difference. (One kind is capable of genuine humility; the other is not.)

Lastly (I'll let your mother tell you all the rest), marry someone who makes you laugh—deeply and often. Laughter is not trivial. Laughter in marriage can heal wounds, deflate our self-righteousness and bridge the little gaps of alienation that grow up between people who live close together. He doesn't have to be funny, but he has to have a sense of humor (which isn't the same thing). Besides, Julie, you are very funny, so all he really has to be is a good audience. If a man takes life too seriously to laugh a lot, he doesn't take it seriously enough.

A final word—don't be in a hurry! If you marry while you are still a girl, you have a good chance of marrying someone who will always be a boy. And it might be, though I don't think it is the norm, that you will not marry at all. The less you feel you *have* to get married, the more likely you are to find someone who will make you glad you did. Which is how I feel about my own marriage to your mom. I hope, Julie, for as much for you.

Love, Papa

TWENTY-SIX

When I Grow Up...

Papa, what should we be
when we grow up?

Dear children,

THERE IS SO MUCH I WOULD LIKE TO SAY ABOUT THIS and yet so much that I know you can only discover for yourself.

Let me start by saying it doesn't matter very much what you do to make the money it takes to stay alive. It matters tremendously, however, *who you are*.

Sounds just like a parent, doesn't it? "Be a good person." "Be nice or you won't have any friends." "Don't crack your knuckles; it will make them big."

Parents often say these kinds of boring things because they have learned a few things the hard way. They have learned that a job doesn't tell you who you are, doesn't explain why we are here on earth, doesn't teach you how to be a friend, doesn't—in most cases—give meaning to life or touch on things which last forever.

What *does* last forever? you may ask. You do. I do. Everyone does. God made you once and that essential *you* will never die, even though your body will. Many people don't believe that anymore. It sounds embarrassingly unscientific. My response is, render unto science that which is science's. Much more exists than is dreamed of in science's philosophy.

Because you last forever, this question of what you are going to be is much more crucial than you realize. What you will *be*, you will be for eternity. By comparison, the job or jobs you do for a few years pale into insignificance.

Where can we turn to find what we should and can be? I think you can guess what I would say. We turn to the person who made us, to the one who knows how we work. The Bible tells us throughout its pages who we are and who we can and should be. It is not a collection of finger-shaking rules. It is simply a realistic description of what the facts are.

One of the many places in the Bible that gives me a start on knowing what I want to be is Psalm 15. It doesn't say it all, but gives me more than enough to work on for the next few days. It starts with a question: "O LORD, who may abide in Thy tent? Who may dwell on Thy holy hill?" (v. 1, NASB). It asks, what kind of people does it give God pleasure to be with?

The answer, I think, is part of how God himself would answer *your* question about what you should be: "He who walks with integrity, works righteousness, and speaks truth in his heart" (v. 2, NASB). That's quite an answer, more than I could fully understand in ten lifetimes, much less explain in one letter.

But there's more. He "has no slander on his tongue, . . . does his neighbor no wrong and casts no slur on his fellow man." Later it says, he "keeps his oath even when it hurts" (vv. 3-4, NIV).

This is someone you can count on, someone who tells the truth even if it causes trouble, someone who will do what is best for others, and not just for himself or herself.

This is what you "should be" when you grow up. It comes

from knowing God, the originator of all good things. This is what it means to be a success in life. Money, fame and earthly power are, by comparison, mere toys and rattles.

One last thing. Don't spend too much time worrying about what you are *going* to be. Think about what you *are*. Because what you are going to be is being decided right now. You are making choices. You are, consciously or unconsciously, choosing what is important to you. You are deciding whether or not you want to live on God's holy hill (a place which exists in the poorest ghetto as much as in the nicest church—it's anywhere there are people who want to walk with integrity and work righteousness).

And as you decide these things, you are deciding what you are and will be. The decisions you make will matter today, tomorrow and forever. I love you guys, and I pray that God will help you to choose wisely.

Love, Papa

TWENTY-SEVEN

Jobs That
Let You Live

Okay, Papa. We know that life
is more than a job,
but jobs and careers are also
part of life. What kind
do you think we should have?

Dear children,

YOU'RE RIGHT. ONCE THE ISRAELITES GOT OUT OF THE wilderness, even God gave up on dropping food out of the sky. A living does have to be earned, and it's important to think about how to do that.

I'm going to skip the obvious stuff. Your school placement counselors can tell you about evaluating your skills and your preferences and your personality and matching those with appropriate careers. There must be some value in those things, though I never heard of anybody who actually ended up doing what those placement tests told them they should like to do.

My junior-high tests said I was suited to be a forest ranger. Looking at it now, the only way I would like that is if they put me in an isolated watchtower with an extensive library of books, a well-stocked refrigerator and didn't bother me about forest fires. If you hear of a ranger job like that, let me know.

Instead of talking about skills and interests I want to talk about a few basic principles to apply to any career and any long-term job. (Of course, short term you may have to do almost *anything*. I was Mr. Trash for a few years and don't regret it at all. But that's another story.)

Principle number one is look for a career that exercises as many aspects of your humanity as possible. You are a blend of many different things: intellect, imagination, emotion, spirit, character, personality, body and so on. These are the things that make you wonderfully human. Any job that lets you use only one or two of these detracts from your being all that you were created to be.

Second, look for a job or career that is compatible with the many other *you*s besides the one that earns a paycheck. When an adult is asked, "What are you?" it is normal to answer by naming your job. But there are in reality many *you*s. Besides a wage earner, you are potentially a husband or wife, a church member, a father or mother, a volunteer in the community, a museum-goer, an amateur athlete, a journal writer, a reader of books— a general explorer of life.

If your job threatens or is threatened by all those things, you likely don't have a genuinely good job, no matter how much money or prestige it may carry with it. Remember, you only have so many hours to live. A job which demands too many of those hours is literally costing you your life. It had better give you more than mere money in exchange.

We tend to think that jobs pay us something. We need to ask, however, what *we* are paying for that job. Time is one of the most precious things we have. Spend it judiciously. Henry Thoreau said that most people think someone who has inherited a farm is lucky. Thoreau wondered whether that farm wasn't likely to become a ball and chain instead. If we must work all our lives in order to maintain our possessions, who owns whom? No matter what career you end up in, ask yourself every so often,

"Do I have a job, or does my job have me?"

Lastly, a really good job has eternal consequences. It gives you the potential, at least, for working with things that last forever. The only things I know like that in this world are human beings. Parts of us are as fragile and transient as the winter snow, but other parts were made in the forges of eternity and will never pass away. If you can touch those parts, if you can shape them even slightly for the better, then you have done the most valuable thing a human creature can do.

Some jobs lend themselves to this more than others. My own is one. But actually this *can* be true of any job no matter how inconspicuous or unsought. Where I work there is a fellow named Keith. He has one of those jobs not many people seek. But if you took a survey of the people who have passed through that institution over the last twenty years, asking them who they remember as an encourager, as someone who got them to smile when they least felt like it, who went out of his way to give them a hand, who reminded them that life was okay when they were having their doubts, more of them would name Keith than anyone. His job description includes nothing of eternal consequence. The way he *does* his job is filled with it.

By these criteria, many of the "good jobs" in our society *aren't*. You will have to decide for yourself what your own criteria are. My guess is they will change substantially between the ages of twenty-five and thirty-five. By then your first new car will have turned to rust, and the second one won't be quite the thrill the first one was. At least I hope not.

Love, Papa

TWENTY-EIGHT

When I Was Your Age...

What were you like, Papa, when you were a kid?

Dear children,

SMART, OBEDIENT, CUTE, LOVABLE, TALENTED, KIND and humble. Next question?

Okay, so maybe I wasn't all those things. It's hard to say what I was like because you can't be sure that what you remember is what you really were. Besides, I was a kid for a long time and I wasn't exactly the same at one time as I was at another.

I'll tell you a few things I think I remember about myself and you can ask Grandma Nita if they're right or not.

I remember thinking a lot as a kid. I wondered about how the world worked and where I fit in to it all. When I was three or four we lived on a lemon orchard in Ventura, California. They cleared out part of the orchard and moved in a house from somewhere else. The house was up on big jacks—big, greasy jacks. I remember looking at that grease and wondering what it would feel like to be a black kid. I didn't wonder for long. Instead, I took big gobs of the grease and started rubbing it all over my face and arms and hands. I went home to show your grandma so she would know what it was like to have a black child. Turned out, she wasn't interested. She had this prejudice against grease.

I also thought a lot when I was a kid about right and wrong. I had this great desire, as I remember, to do the right thing. Part of it was because maybe I was afraid of getting in trouble. I remember when I was in second grade, when we lived in Wheeler, Texas, and my teacher sent me on an errand of some kind. As I walked by the principal's office, I looked in the door and saw a frightening sight. I can still see the principal with a big, long paddle swacking the butt of a yelping kid. For some reason I was shocked down to my sagging socks. I remember saying slowly to myself as I edged away, "I'm never going to do anything that will let them do that to me."

But I don't think it was just being afraid of being punished. I think I really *wanted* to do what was right. I wanted to be on Jesus' side and to defeat evil if I could. Sometimes I got mixed up. When I was in third grade, there were these older kids, fourth and fifth graders, who were sort of my heroes. They could run fast and were tough and could talk to girls without getting cooties and were just generally about everything a kid could want to be.

One Saturday I was walking along the banks of the creek down by the ball field when I came to the swimming hole. You won't believe what I saw. There were those guys swimming—NAKED! They were skinny-dipping, and I was shocked. Swinging on the rope, jumping off the banks, with their clothes laying right there where God could send somebody along to steal their pants so as to punish them.

I was very disillusioned. I couldn't believe that guys I had admired so much could do something so . . . so . . . so, well, *bad*. Looking back on it now, I don't think they did anything bad at all. But at that age, for me, being anywhere outside without clothes on was about as frightening a notion as I could come up with and it just had to be, well, bad.

I also thought a lot about God and about heaven and hell and about what would happen to me if I died. I remember thinking for a while that I was going to *have* to be a preacher because only preachers could possibly be good enough not to go to hell. And I thought when I was a preacher, I would preach *every* sermon on hell because what could be more important than scaring people away from it?

Later I learned it wasn't my being good that determined whether God loved me. And I decided I could probably get to heaven without being a preacher, which was a great relief. But I never have stopped thinking about God and the world and where I fit in to everything. I hope I never do.

I also remember being sort of a softhearted kid. I didn't like things dying and even worse was the idea of their suffering. We used to fish a lot when we lived in Santa Barbara, and I can remember feeling sorry for the fish. I must have been the only fisherman ever who hoped he wouldn't catch anything.

Actually, I did want to catch fish. It was just that when I did I never knew whether to keep them or throw them back. All the other kids kept theirs, even if they threw them away later. I thought I should probably keep mine too, but I would lay them beside me and watch their mouths opening and closing and feel their eyes looking at me. And they were so quiet, of course, and I felt like they were saying, "What did we ever do to you? Why are you doing this to us? Help! We can't breathe!"

And a lot of times I would take the fish after it had been sitting there awhile, when no on else was looking, and throw it back into the water. And sometimes they would jerk their tails and disappear in the water and I would feel good again. But other times they would just float there belly-up, and I would feel like a killer and yet would have lost the fish too.

The same is true with birds and BB guns. When I was ten or eleven I went shooting with my friend Roger on his grandparents' little ranch. Roger was shooting all these birds. Whenever he gave the gun to me, I would miss on purpose. I couldn't tell him I didn't want to kill birds, so I just made sure I never hit anything.

He kept making fun of me for being such a bad shot. Finally I got mad and decided to shoot one just to shut him up. I remember it was a bluebird. I aimed right at it this time and knocked it out of the tree. We ran up to it and it was flopping around on the ground. I shot it again to put it out of its misery, but it still didn't die, so I had to shoot it four more times before it stopped flapping. I felt as bad after that as maybe I've ever felt about anything. I knew I had done something I felt was wrong just because I was afraid of what someone else would think of me. I've tried in my life not to make that mistake again.

When I got older I guess I became a little bit of a loner. Not that I didn't have good friends or love my family, but just that I liked to be alone more than some people do. Your mom thinks it happened because we moved so much (sixteen times before I was sixteen), but I don't know if that's true. My guess is I just liked to think and most people do that best by themselves. I kept thinking about the things I had always thought about and a lot of new things besides. And, like I said before, I'm still thinking.

That's a little bit of what I think I was like as a kid. It's now apparent to me that each of you is like me in some ways. Matthew, you seem to think about a lot of things. Julie, you seem more concerned than most kids about what's right and wrong in the world. And you, Nate, have a tender heart, and I hope you always do.

You know, it hadn't occurred to me when I started this letter that each of you is something like what I was. But I'm glad to have discovered it. I hope you are glad too.

Love, Papa

TWENTY-NINE

A Letter to
My Child-to-Be

Near the end of writing and collecting
these letters, during which I of course thought
a lot about our three children, we discovered
that I was thinking too small.
God perhaps figured that if I had so much
wisdom for children that I needed to
enshrine it in writing, then surely it would
be a shame for me not to have another
opportunity to exercise it.

God is like this. Watch out for him.

Dear yet-to-be-born one,

*OH, YOU LITTLE BUNDLE OF SERENDIPITY! YOU EVI-*dence of heavenly wit! Outfoxer of overconfident plans! You complicator, gift, challenge, reward! (You are these things and much more.) I did not see you coming. Must have been looking the other way. I don't recall getting your letter. Did you phone ahead?

You are good for me. You remind me that I am not in absolute control of my own life. Absolute control is for dictators. Those who love life do so partly for its unpredictability. If there are no surprises there is no freshness. You are freshness to us.

You are also a test. I have gone on and on about many values in these letters. Do I really believe them? More important, do I genuinely live them? I have made it admirably clear that I believe money relatively unimportant. But, truthfully, didn't part of me see us maybe getting a little bit ahead in the next few years? Didn't I contemplate your mother working more (getting paid for a change, that is) as your brothers and sister made their way through school?

But what, you force me to ask, do I mean by "ahead"? Who is ahead and who is behind in this world? That can only be determined by knowing where it is we are headed, knowing the destination against which ahead and behind are measured. And when I think about it that way, I can only be glad for you. Everything in my understanding of why we are here and where we are going tells me that you put us further ahead. I thank you for that reminder.

In these letters (which are for you too) I have talked about the importance of infusing our lives with eternal things. Nothing is more eternal than you. You are evidence that God is still interested in this world, that he hasn't given up on us. God had another thought about the possibilities of life, and you are that thought. Our lives are inevitably richer, as they always are when we touch that which lasts forever.

At this point, I cannot quite envision you. It has been a long time since there has been such newness in the house. I try to remember what it was like with your brothers and sister and (mercifully perhaps) cannot fully recollect. I know I will have to do in my forties things that were tiring even when I was in my twenties. But that's okay; it will get me off the couch.

Though my knowledge of you is only general (smaller as you are now than the fingers which type these words), my hopes for you are specific. I wish for you a knowledge and love of your Creator. I wish for you someone to love and be loved by. I wish for you things to do which will give your life meaning. I wish for you friends and family and a community of faith. I wish for you the ability to mourn with those who mourn and laugh with those who laugh.

Yes, I wish you much laughter. I must confess that right now, at this point in our lives together, the thought of you makes us laugh, maybe a little nervously. You must forgive me if part of me wonders about all this. You are, you must remember, still a new idea. I assure you—when I first see you, *all* of me will be glad.

Your old-but-loving Papa

An Afterword to Parents

If these letters have stirred any juices in you, I encourage you to write your own. It doesn't matter how old your children are. They may be very young or grown and gone—or even not quite here yet. Speak your mind and heart. (If you aren't a parent and won't be, write to someone else—everyone is someone's child.)

Try to write *through* your life. In his fine autobiographies, Frederick Buechner advises us to listen to our lives, to seek those patterns and rhythms of meaning that we often miss in the living of life but can discover on looking back. Our lives are filled with significance—if only we have eyes to see.

And nothing is more significant than high values lived out in the details of our lives. These can be shared with our children. Be sure, however, to include your failures. Children understand woundedness and failure because they feel them often themselves. Perseverance in trying to do right is more compelling than unblemished saintliness.

I must admit, however, that I didn't start out to write letters about values. I discovered I was doing that much later. Write about anything you feel strongly about, anything that has a touch of passion in it, anything that has been long lingering in your bones, and you will see that you too are writing about values.

Tell stories. We love to hear stories because they are mostly about human beings surviving trouble. And we all need the encouragement that comes from discovering that others have been afflicted as we and have found a way to the other side. In stories are pain and struggle and failure, but also laughter and wisdom and grace. Your stories will have these things as much as anyone's, and you do not have to be good with words to tell them powerfully.

A final word of advice—write letters and tell stories that are ultimately affirming. Don't settle scores or preach old sermons. Children are flesh of our flesh and bone of our bone. Their lives are and will be difficult—as yours may have been—and they need all the encouragement they can get. They might also need a kick in the seat, but there are many to give them that. Speak to them words of encouragement and love. They will learn, thereby, to speak such words to others.

In writing on what you care about to those you love, you will enrich the world eternally.

Daniel Taylor